Acknowledgements

I want to thank all the people who sent me photographs. I apologise in advance if there are any mistakes and misplaced names and if the dates aren't all absolutely accurate. I was delighted that a great many former pupils and teachers were so enthusiastic and generous with their contributions. Several people responded to requests for memories with their own memorable stories. I am grateful to all of them and to John Nicholson in particular.

Thank you to the reference librarians at the Ewart Public Library, Dumfries for the access to the Minutes of Dumfries Education Committee and of the Dryfesdale School Board. Also to John Gair, former history teacher, on whose early research I was able to base my own.

I particularly want to thank Mr Graham Herbert, the school's Rector, and his staff for their kindness, encouragement and hospitality; Mac Creedon, printer and publisher, for his help and infinite patience; my family and friends for their support and unfailing interest and finally to all the staff and pupils, past and present, for making Lockerbie Academy such a great school.

Author's Foreword

I was born and brought up in Dumfriesshire where I attended Lochmaben Primary School and Lockerbie Academy.

Some time ago I decided to write a book about my primary school when I discovered through researching my family history that the school had been responsible for educating four generations of the Wilson Family.

That book was a success and that spurred me on to write about my secondary school.

Lockerbie Academy has featured greatly in the lives of the Wilsons as well as in my mother's family the Shennans. Furthermore some of my extended family were taught in Lockerbie.

The first family member to attend the school in Lockerbie was my grandfather, David Edward Wilson, the son of a tenant farmer. He left Lochmaben Primary, age 12, in 1899 to continue his studies at Lockerbie alongside his brother, Robert (nos 1655, 1656)

David was bright and went up to Kilmarnock to board there and study engineering. He then secured work with the Beardmore Company at Dalmuir on the Clyde. He worked on submarines during World War One, but after the war he returned with his family to Lochmaben and to the farm where he had been born. Unfortunately he suffered from ill health and died there prematurely in1939.

No.				Name		D.o.B			Father/Parent	Occupation	Address
1633	99	9	25	William Foster		85	12	28	John Jas.	Bicycle Maker	Main Street L
1634	..	.	27	Maggie Henderson		95	5	24	Alex:	Constable	Police Station
1635	.	.	.	Effie Heron		94	10	26	Henry	Engine Driver	Caledonian Pl
1636	..	..	6	Robert Edgar		87	3	2	Robert	Plate Layer	Sawedpholm
1637		10	2	Euphemia Aitken		88	6	22	Thos	Farmer	Lockerbie
1638	.	..	3	Mary J. Macintosh		95	6	25	Wm	Shepherd	Townhead, Loc
1639	..	8	29	Mary Porteous		84	9	3	Richd	Farmer	19 Bruce St. Loc
1640	..	10	5	William Carruthers		89	7	31	Jane		Dryfebridge
1641	..	.	..	Margaret Walker		93	11	5	Jas Petrie	Baker	37 Sydney Pl
1642	..	.	..	Jane Carruthers		92	5	12	Jane		Dryfebridge
1022	99	8	22	Margt Mackenzie		Readmitted					
1643	..	10	14	May Mitchell		93	8	14	Mrs Jas Mitchell		110 High Street, Loc
1644	..	..	.	Mary Robertson		94	1	5	Joseph	Saddler	4 Brewery Yard
1645	.	.	23	Rachel Thorburn		86	2		Mrs Thorburn		Farmers Hill
1646	.	9	6	James Currie		93	11	28	James	Vanman	2 Main St. Lo
1647	.	9	16	Jeannie Inglis		95	2	14	Robt	Surfaceman	Caledonian Pl
1648	98	8	31	Agnes Telfer		92	11	4	Thos	Brakesman	33 Bridge Street
1649	99	10	17	James Robson		91	12	26	Joseph	Saddler	4 Brewery Yd.
1650	..	.	16	Richard Inman		94	7	20	Thos	Signal Fitter	Caledonian Bdgs
1651	..	.	23	Agnes Campbell		86	12	6	Mrs Agnes	Dairy Woman	Sloda Hill
1652	..	.	.	William Campbell		89	1	2	..	..	..
1653	99	11	12	Lizzie Carruthers		93	4	25	William Carruthers		Main Street
1654	99	11	12	Lily Renwick		95	4	21	Jas. Renwick		Castlehill C
1655	..	11	13	Robert Andrew Wilson		86	6	4	Andrew	Farmer	Effie, Lochma
1656	..	..	..	David Edward Wilson		87	4	4			
1657	..	..	..	Agnes Robson		86	11	13	Joseph	Saddler	4 Brewery Yar
1658	..	..	29	John Anderson		91	8	5	Andrew Anderson		Townhead St. L

Admittance Register 1899

Education in Lockerbie

Early days

No doubt there were many forms of education in Lockerbie and its environs before the 18th century. Most likely, in common with other Scottish parishes, these would be run by the church, with often the minister serving as the schoolmaster or dominie.

A former pupil, Max Scott, kept a diary and in it he recorded what he had been told about the school by Miss Hunter who taught History in the 30s and 40s. These dates have not been verified.

1438	Commencement of schooling in Lockerbie;
1750	School was moved to Myreside along Beckton Road to make the school more central for pupils from outlying areas; Before 1751 Robert Kennedy was the dominie;
1757	Walter Irving appointed dominie;
1803	Wage of dominie was £16.13/4d;
1806	Death of Walter Irving after 49 years of teaching;
1815	Death of James Davidson school dominie;
1815	Probably when Ferguson became dominie;
1834	Death of William Dobie age 80 who taught almost until his death.

The 18th century

The Old Statistical Account for Dumfriesshire was written between 1791 and 1799. In the section on Dryfesdale, there is described an established parochial school, but the author noted that the small amount of salary and fees did not encourage schoolmasters in Scotland – some things never change! There were also several private schools in the parish.

The 19th century

In Pigot's Directory* for Lockerbie in 1827 the parochial school situated at the top of Bridge Street and the headmaster, Alexander Ferguson are mentioned. There were other: "Academies and schools" in the parish – a boarding school run by the Rev. William Dunbar at Applegarth and a Ladies' School in the High Street run by Agnes Gillespie. Simeon Blackstock and James Hawkins both of the High Street are also mentioned - presumably they were tutors.

By the time the New Statistical Account had been written in 1836 the parochial School and six privately endowed schools were established. The account records that: " Everyone over the age of 15 can read and write and generally around eight young men attend classes in Edinburgh or Glasgow University." Girls were barred from university at this time.

Slater's directory* in 1852 mentions The Rev Dunbar's school as well as Ferguson's parochial school.

According to local historian, John Gair, the Parish School was situated at the head of Bridge Street in 1794. An extension was built in the 19th century along the Corrie Road and the whole group of buildings is known as Ferguson Place after the old dominie.

In his "Recollections of Lockerbie", the local worthie, Thomas Henderson, wrote about: "The house now known as Ravenswood was a one storey building and used as a private school."

In 1843 The Free Church of Scotland was established, having broken away from the Church of Scotland. After this "Great Disruption", The Free Church School was established in Lockerbie. The building became used as a drill hall in 1875 and during the First World War was an army hospital.

The Free Church School

In 1846 pupil teachers were introduced and this gave way to women coming into the profession. A pupil teacher was a bright child who helped the class teacher, being responsible for small groups within the class, and later took examinations with a view to becoming a teacher.

There was also Mr Stewart's School situated where the old Episcopal Church School stood and in 1873 there is mention, in the minutes of the Board of Dryfesdale School, of other schools run by Miss Dobie and Mrs Henderson. Presumably these would have been "Dame Schools". These schools were found all over Scotland and run by ladies who usually had no formal qualifications, but would give some basic instruction in reading and writing to youngsters.

The log book of Dryfesdale Public School opens: "October 14th 1873 the Public School (late Parish School) of Lockerbie, was opened today by Robert S Muir, late of Pulteney Town Academy." He was to be the new Headmaster. The site chosen was at Townhead and the roll was 305 pupils.

The laying of the Foundation stone took place on October 30th 1874 with a masonic procession. The Queen's Anthem was sung and a prayer was read by the chaplain. Some coins were placed in the stone's cavity and the band played "Hail Masonry". This was followed by a masonic procedure laying the stone then Psalm 100 was sung by the choir. Wine and oil were poured on the stone and the band then played the Masons' Anthem. The Right Worshipful Master (Brother Arthur Johnstone Douglas of Lockerbie of Quhytewoollen Lodge) gave an address. The Representative of the School Board replied and after a benediction the choir sang "Rule Britannia".

In Victorian times, the Church and the masons were powerful groups and they had a strong influence on education – who taught and what was taught. Some members of both groups

*Pigot's and Slater's directories are books containing lists of businesses

became members of the School Board and this itself was much more influential than its modern equivalent.

The Education (Scotland) Act of 1872 had led to the formation of Dryfesdale School Board and the minutes record that on January 5th 1875 : "All the schools amalgamated today." The official opening was in October. Control of the school system was now taken from the Church of Scotland and taken over by the Scottish Education Department

There were to be 3 departments - the Infants under Miss Kidd; the Junior Dept under Mr Cunningham and the Senior Department (pupils over the age of 13) to be taken by the headmaster, Mr Muir. There were 6 teachers , 4 pupil teachers and 526 pupils in attendance. The school year ran from !st November to 31st October when exams and the annual inspection took place.

A leaving certificate was introduced in 1888 to set national standards and was not replaced until 1962!

Concern over the materials for the building were reported: "The contractor for the mason work should not to be tied down to Corncockle Stone, but should have the option of taking the Locharbriggs Hard or North End Sandstone, the architect (James Barbour) to be satisfied of this."

Schooling was now compulsory from 5 to 13. It was not free and some parents were often summoned to appear in front of the Board for either non payment of fees or for the non attendance of their children.

The minutes record the first parent called for non-attendance in March 1874: "... didn't send his son. He said that he couldn't pay the fees and so was referred to the parochial board." No proceedings were made that time, but in May there was the first prosecution of a parent for not sending his two children to school.

By 1903 serious attempts were made to make pupils attend more punctually and regularly. There would be an incentive. Those who complied would receive each week a "pictorial card". The cost of these cards was to be taken from the sum for attendance prizes: "Cost would be between 6/- and 10/6 for 1000 and so 10.000 could be bought."

Today schools have to report attendance figures nationally and schools are set targets to lower the numbers of truancies. Teachers have to think up all sorts of "motivators" such as special treats for pupils who collect stamps for good attendance, all in line with positive behaviour policies. I doubt, however, that some of today's youngsters would be better attenders if they knew they would receive "pictorial cards".

An evening school was also established : "The Continuation School ...is a boon to any district." Sixty pupils were enrolled in 1897. Two years later there were 78 and 9 subjects were taught: beekeeping and crook making included.

The opening of more buildings took place in 1897 which coincided with the establishment of a Secondary Department.

The catchment area was and still is large. The board wrote to the General Manager of the Caledonian Railway Company regarding the stoppage of trains for use of Ecclefechan pupils and managed to negotiate the stopping of the train at Ecclefechan at 9.34 am. Again this shows the power of the School Board in this period.

Bankshill and Kettleholm Home Guard outside the now demolished wooden building of Lockerbie Academy.
Included are Richard Common, Robert Black, Bobby McBride, John Spence and Mr Campbell.

The 20th century

The school leaving age was now 14 and by 1903 the school was able to achieve the status of a Higher Grade School and the name Lockerbie Academy was first used. The school census showed 542 children in attendance. Class teaching was giving way to subject teaching which is now the norm for secondary schools. Another innovation was reporting to parents formally. Reports on pupils in the Higher Grade Department were to be sent out every quarter to give an indication of progress (or otherwise) and a summary of the work completed.

In 1905 the Board wanted to purchase another field to make a bigger play area which confirms that the school was still expanding. Mr Sanders (Chairman of the Board) was so frustrated with the deadlock concerning its purchase that he decided to go ahead and pay for it himself. At least they named it after him.

The school became a 5 year school in 1919 and a wooden building used for Art and Music was added. This can be seen in the Home Guard Photo.

Educational policy changes made by Dumfries County Council later, however, led to pupils having to transfer to Dumfries Academy if they wished to continue for 4th and 5th years. This was not possible for all able pupils as the costs of travel and / or accommodation had to be met by parents.

An exceptional pupil, Jean Gardiner, was one of those whose parents couldn't afford for her to continue her education at Dumfries She was awarded prize certificates and books throughout the decade 1922-32 for General Excellence, Merit and General Proficiency and for subjects as diverse as Science,

History, Latin, Maths, English, Geography and Book Keeping; essays in French; the Lady Buchanan Jardine Prize for Sewing and in 1931 the Burns Club First Prize. She would have been an obvious candidate for university. Jean was at least able to remain at Lockerbie where she studied Secretarial Work and Spanish.

The cost of staying on at school affected my own mother who, despite her teachers' pleas to stay on, was determined to leave, partly because her own mother was by then an impoverished widow. Desperate to leave and have proof for her teachers that she had a job, she had seen a notice in the local hardware shop: "Boy wanted"; applied and secured the post! She didn't stay there for long, but she did work for many years at the Post Office Exchange as a telephonist until she married.

In the 1942-43 HMI Report mention is made of the plans for a new art room and better science accommodation. Unfortunately because of WW2 there was not enough money.

The school leaving age was eventually raised to 15 in 1947. Consequently the additional pupils needed more space so temporary classrooms were built.

The Third Statistical account written by the Rev. J C Steen in 1962 described Lockerbie Academy: "As the centre of education in the parish. In the 1960s children over 12 were no longer educated in the country schools and are conveyed daily to Lockerbie."

In 1952 there were 900 pupils and 35 teachers whereas today's ratio is 800 pupils and over 60 teaching staff . A new building phase began in 1957 and in 1962 Lockerbie Academy became a 4 year school, but 2 years later became a 6 year school, allowing fifteen year olds from Langholm, Beattock and Moffat to continue their secondary education to age 18.

The school leaving age was raised yet again in 1972.

Prize Bookplate

Lockerbie Academy (built in the 1960s as it is today)

The primary school was relocated in the old sandstone building facing Townhead Street and the photo below shows primary pupils in 1976 outside their school.

By the mid 1970s the primary became a separate school with its own headmaster, Mr Gordon Paterson, but later in the decade a new primary school was built and the old building taken over as Council offices.

A poem written by Alan Welsh (former English teacher) in 1975 was published in the school magazine, Mosaic. The poem written in Scots reflects on 100 years of the school in Lockerbie. It gives a vivid account of how the children dressed, what they ate, how they got to school and what they were taught.

The 21st Century

The new century with new teaching methods require new premises so in 2007 plans have been drawn up for a new school built under the Public Private Partnership scheme.

This will have high tech facilities including dance and drama studios and will once more amalgamate the primary and secondary schools.

With this change the school is well placed to deal with the challenges of the next hundred years.

NB Whilst excavating the new site, some important archaeological features were discovered. Evidence has been found of an Early Neolithic timber built structure with associated pottery. A later timber- built structure about 7th century AD and a small Bronze Age cemetery have also been found.

Plans for the new school

100 LINES! (WELL, NEARLY) FOR THE CENTENARY

Yestreen I dreamed an unco dream
Methocht I saw a steady stream
O' bairns, frae ilka hoose an' croft
A' dressed in claes their mithers coft.
The knickerbockers ower their knees
On breeks o' homespun or o' frieze,
Ower woollen stockin's, buits wi' tackets
(It maittered nocht aboot the racket)
Or aiblains clogs a' shod wi airn
Whilk were the pride o' ilka bairn.
Wi' ane anither they wad vie
To gar the sparks frae stones to fly.
The lassie ower their dresses wore
An apron or a pinafore,
Wi' stockin's thick and made wi' oos
That mither knitted ben the hoose.
Some had shoon they wore wi' pride
But buits that buttoned up the side
Shod some o' them, gey nearly a',
Yet ilka quean thocht she looked braw.
In winter wi' its bleak cauld days
Some bairns were sewn intil their claes
An' keepit that way till the Spring!
Ye'd hardly credit sic a thing.
But whaur were a' the bairnies gaun,
Some looking feart, some looking' thawn?
Ah weel, I'll answer whit you speir,
A brew new schule's been buildit here
Ilk ane maun gae, there's nae reprieve,
(But they at thirteen years may leave,
An' tak' a job, no' ill to seek,
That payed them one and six a week!)
The dominies were dour an' thrang,
At ilk ane's side a tawse was hang,
They garred the weans learn ilka trick
O' Reading, 'Riting, 'Rithmetic.
An, aiblains, gin they couldna take it,
The stour wad flee frae mony a jaiket.
Ilk class was dull and tinged wi' gloom
Wi' fifty-odd weans to the room
Wi' that lot teachers sune were wabbit,
Nae wonder they were a' sae crabbit!
Nae buses brocht them to the schule
But Shanks' Mare was then the rule
Fower miles some bairnies had to walk
(They rose each morning wi' the cock)
An' fower miles hame again at nicht
In winter it was scarcely licht.
An' yet they cam' in hail or snaw
A wonner they got there ava'.
Some a day's work had dune, nae doot
Afore they even started oot.
For denner, if indeed they'd any,
A bowl of soup wad cost a penny.
For sums they'd use a muckle slate
Their writing gey near copper-plate,
They had to buy the books they read
An' moral tales filled every head

- - - - - - - - - - - - - - - - - - - -

I woke, and sat up in my bed
An' thochts cam' dirlin' through my head.
Projectors, wireless and TV
An' a' the books an' jotters free!
A new schule built wi' ample space!
(Wi' fourteen hunner weans to place).
Noo Shanks' Mare is lang syne dead
They come by bus and car instead.
Yet mony think they've cause to grieve
Till they're sixteen they canna leave
While ithers think the schule is smashin',
Since punishment gaed oot o' fashion!
The biggest class hauds thirty-five
Some teachers ken na they're alive.
An' will the future cause concern?
Will pupils dictate what they'll learn?
Will teachers ha'e to toe the line
An', wistful, sigh for Auld Lang Syne?
Or will it ever come to pass
That fifteen bairns will mak' a class?
But noo, my Muse has taken fricht
Sic things are e'en ayont her sicht.
An' she will bide 'mid rustic scenery
Till wanted for the Bi-Centenary!
(But no' by me!)

A. W.

Poem written by Alan Welsh and published in "MOSAIC" 1975

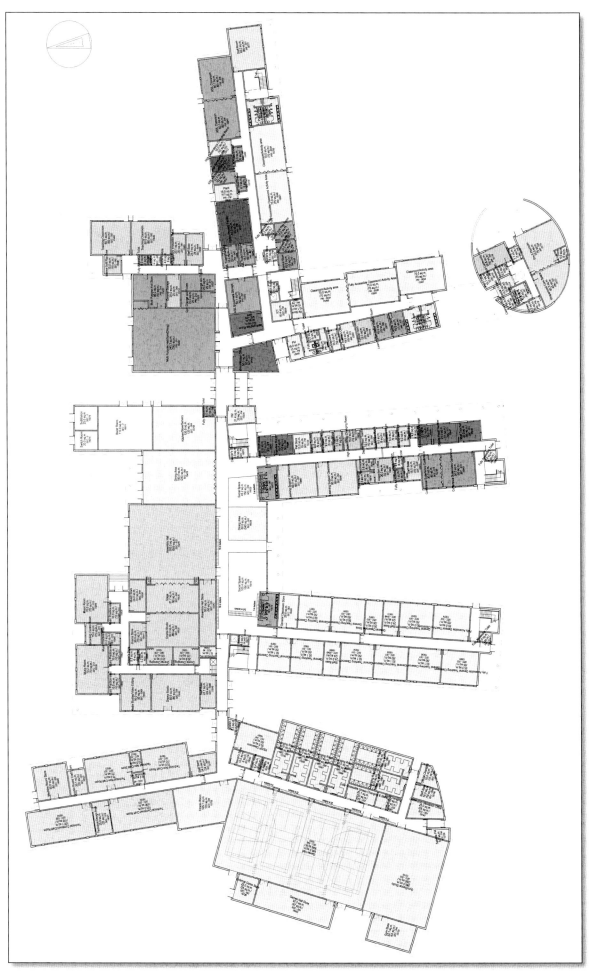

Plans for the new school

Head Teachers and Staff

Alexander Ferguson (1820s-1879)

He was "Auld Curly wi' the Tawse", the headmaster of the old Parochial School who taught in Lockerbie for over 50 years and retired on a pension of £70. Both he and his wife, Jessie Wright, came from farming families. According to GC Kirk writing in 1897 in "Dryfesdale, Various Pen Sketches" : "He was at once calm with dignity and carefulness, and fearful to the boys."

He devoted special attention to English, Latin and Greek, but he is mainly remembered for his extreme use of the belt - the toppit tawse - and the resultant :"Shattered jacket backs." Kirk retells the following illustrative story - a tale of two mothers in the 1840s:

"Mrs J - 'Seeing oor just oorsels twa, hoos your boy getting on wi' his Latin books?'

Mrs F - 'O deed, I dinna ken; I think no ava, for his mind's no in them.'

Mrs J - ' Weel, I may jist say the same o' oor Wullie, but what's his jacket like?'

Mrs F - 'His jacket! I've sic mending! a' chittled wi' the mice seeking his left crumbs o' cheese-and-bread. This while back I mak' him clean his pouches o' moolins when he comes hame frae the schuil, and still they're shattered.'

Mrs J (laughing) - 'Y'er no a bit better than mysel, but I've found oot noo, I was gaein oor Wullie sic a raging the other nicht, and told him I wad burn that pistol o' his, if he wad persist makin' his jacket a target on the hedge to shoot at.'

Little Jean -' O mither, its no the pistol ava! It's the maister's tawse that holes his jacket, for I saw lots o' boys the verra same.'

Mrs F - 'If ever I heard the like o' this, and me blaming the puir, innocent mice!'

Alexander Ferguson (Died 1879)
Headmaster of Dryfesdale Parish School for over 50 years
"Auld curly wi' the tawse"

An old rhyme links Ferguson to Fisher, one of the teachers, and the Reverend Whyte who opened the new school:

> "Curly Fergie keeps a schuil,
> Johnny Fisher teaches,
> Apple Johnny rings the bell,
> And Whyte, the farmer, preaches."

The School Board advertised for: "A headmaster, capable of teaching Classics and Modern Languages at a salary of £200 per annum." There were 46 applicants from whom six were interviewed. One of the candidates was Mr Cunningham from the Free School. He was appointed as second master and paid £140. The third teacher was Mr Fisher (previously assistant at the parish school) paid £70 and the female teacher would receive £65. This was a hundred years before the Equal Pay Act. The board also employed Mrs Henderson of Townhead, Lockerbie as a sewing teacher for the grand salary of £12.12.0d.

Robert Muir (native of Dalbeattie)

1873-1880 was the first Head Master of Dryfesdale Public School, however he was not a well man and in July 1875 he had been granted a spell of absence and a Mr David Thomson deputised for him. According to the minutes of the school board Mr Muir asked for a pay rise in 1876: "Having declined offers of jobs elsewhere." They decided they wanted to keep Mr Muir and offered him £250 annual salary. He died in 1880.

A Maxwell Palmer 1881-1889

One very important decision made by Mr Palmer and the School Board in 1886 was to install flushing toilets!

Peter Malcolm 1889-1923

By this time the Headmaster's salary was £230. He had 3 assistants - Messers Wright, Hair and Fisher at £100 each; and assistants, Miss Malcolm at £90, Miss Curdie at £70, Miss Readdie at £70 and Miss Irving at £65. There were also 8 pupil teachers who were paid £140 in total. One wonders why there were so many different salaries. In 1908 Mr Malcolm was looking for a science master. The post was advertised at a salary of £120 rising to £150. Applications with 8 copies of testimonials were to be lodged with David McJerrow, the solicitor (and no photocopiers in those days).

Under Mr Malcolm's leadership, huge changes were made to the curriculum, the buildings and the teaching methods. He must be given credit for heading the school so well in a time of great change which included the demands made by the First World War.

Mr Malcolm must have been delighted with the 1900 HMI report - a headteacher's dream - which declared : "High levels of attainment; uniform proficiency; no weak subject anywhere;

interesting and stimulating lessons in Nature Knowledge; intelligent style of Reading and Recitation is practised; in each stage of Mathematics the work is very accurate; knowledge of Latin grammar is unusually complete; In French, translation and composition are very correct and facile; useful instruction in Shorthand is given with success and in dealing with Science the teachers show skill in combining clear exposition with illustrative experiment; carefully devised scheme of Cookery and Household Economy ; specimens of Sewing submitted are uniformly excellent; the interest which boys take in Woodwork is evidence of skilful teaching ; In both Physical and Military Drill for the supervision of which a competent instructor is retained the classes make a successful appearance; the merit of Singing is a characteristic of the school and musical instruction in the highest classes is very advanced. The combination of vigour and skill with good nature and forbearance shown in conducting the senior school again calls for favourable notice." The Inspector declared that the upper department be recognised as a separate secondary school.

It was in this year my grandfather received his merit certificate. It is wonderful to think that he benefited from these superb teachers.

Muir Burns 1923-1930 (see staff photo 1920s)

Rector Burns headed the school during the lean and hungry '20s.

On April 1st 1926, however, he presented Miss Margaret Rioch MA with a: "Handsome attaché case as a parting gift". She was going to take up a new post at Inverurie.

A month later he presented Miss Winifred Niven , the infant mistress, with a solid silver cake stand on the occasion of her approaching marriage.

He praised Miss Niven's "faithfulness and ability with which she had discharged her duties" and referred to the general regret at her leaving the profession (Female teachers were obliged to leave their posts on marriage.) She, in turn, referred to the: "Fine spirit of harmony which permeated the staff". All of which seems to imply a benevolent headship.

Robert Hamilton (from Langholm) 1930-1943

Within a week of starting at the school there was a problem with the drains being choked. Mr Hamilton's sense of humour shines through in the log: "Boys' closets inaccessible except by boat"!

The wireless made its first appearance for school use under his headship.

When WW2 broke out in 1939 the school delayed opening for a week. There was much to do. Evacuees from Glasgow had to be accommodated and timetabled. The HMI report of 1942/3 is quite good, but the HMI notes that pupils answered questions well on recent work, but failed to recall earlier topics perhaps this was due to the huge amount of change in staffing. He notes, however, that the head teacher is retiring soon after a period of duty extended because of the war. "His

service to education has been long and distinguished, and his fine influence and organizing ability have been most valuable during the disturbed period through which the school is passing".

Johnstone Hetherington 1944-1957

(staff photo 1946/47)

Mr J Hetherington, by all accounts, was a popular headmaster (Mr Matthew Miller was appointed temporary rector in September 1957 following Mr Hetherington's illness.) Unfortunately Mr Hetherington died on 13th September and six days later Mr Gordon the deputy rector and English teacher also died.

Alexander Simpson 1958-1964

(staff photo 1962)

Mr Simpson was rector when Ordinary Grade courses were introduced in 1962 and when the school became a full 6 year school.

William Anderson 1964-1980

(staff photo 1975)

William Anderson came from Kirkcudbright Academy and was known as Bugs Bunny because of his prominent front teeth no doubt. Two major changes took place under Mr Anderson's rector ship. In 1976 The Parents' Association was formed and in the same year the Primary Department became a separate school under headmaster Gordon Paterson.

Drew Blake 1980-1996 (staff photo 1990)

Drew became Rector in 1980. He'd taught at Langholm, Kelso, Oban and in his native Kilmarnock. He said that his enduring memory of Lockerbie was the establishment of the Syracuse Scholarship. Because 35 Syracuse students had been killed in the aircraft explosion in 1988 it was decided that 35 student scholarships would be offered to pupils from the countries involved. Lockerbie was to be allocated a further two scholarships.

Pupils have to submit essays from which a short leet is drawn. After meetings in London with Syracuse representatives the final interviews are held in Lockerbie. Initially there was some apprehension about students postponing their entrance to British Universities and "disrupting their education". This fear was totally unfounded, but this was before "gap years" were de rigeur. The scholarship continues and one student , Erin McLauchlin, decided to continue her studies at the university after the session ended. She graduated from Syracuse with Honours in History in 2007 and is presently studying for another degree in the States.

Mr Graham Herbert (1996 - present)

Graham became rector in 1996. In 2003, the 15th anniversary of the Pan Am disaster, Graham was awarded the Syracuse University's Chancellor's Medal for Exceptional Achievement as thanks for his unstinting work honouring the lost students and maintaining the link between the two communities.

One indication of Mr Herbert's successful leadership is the excellent HMIe Report of 2003 on Lockerbie Academy. The following is a summary of that report.

We judged the following to be very good

- Climate and relationships
- Equality and fairness
- Curricular and vocational guidance
- Organisation and use of resources and space
- School management of finances

- Structure of the curriculum
- Pastoral care
- Learning support
- Leadership
- Staff review and development

We judged the following to be good

- Expectations and promoting achievement
- Partnership with parents, the School Board and the community
- Reporting pupils' progress
- Staffing
- Provision of resources
- Implementation of legislation relating to SEN and disabilities
- Effectiveness and deployment of staff with additional responsibilities
- Self-evaluation
- Planning for improvement
- Monitoring progress and achievement

We judged the following to be fair

- Accommodation and facilities

We judged the following to be unsatisfactory

- No aspects were found to be in this category.

Graham has overseen the introduction of a school website and is currently involved in the plans for the new school.

Dave Wilson, Drew Blake, Hugh Young and students Katherine Grant and Fiona Griffin

Teaching Staff

In the second edition of the school magazine, "The Lockardian" in 1929 several teachers are mentioned by name and in an article about the school in 1889 a Miss Malcolm in the Infants' department is mentioned. She may have been related to the headmaster. The initials of the teachers of 1929 were:-

Introducing the Staff.

Despite the popular belief that life at school is dull, it is not really so black as it is painted. In the morning we assemble in the hall for a short service. The choir is led by the Jovial Artistic Warbler. The lesson is read by a master with Majestic Bearing. When this is finished we disperse to the tune of a Merry Waltz, what time the doors are opened by an Affable Workman. As We Throng along the corridor we hear a Neat Modest Blonde (or should it be Brunette?) discoursing on and writing Numbers and Moods on a Blackboard. In another corner of the school, while under a Jocose and Capable Taskmaster, we hear at certain times Notes Of Harmony from the hall, and sometimes Loud Shouting and occasionally Light Stepping. In our walk round the corridors we may meet a Grand Methodical Historian collecting revenue. The mathematical section is conducted by one who might have been a Doctor of Divinity instead of holding forth on Diabolical Deductions; there is also a Jupiter of Gigantic Muscles who inspires awe wherever he goes. In the Modern Room you make the acquaintance of Molière and Racine; and Recipes for Cakes arrive once a week in a Modern Rover. These three are frequently seen on the golf course, where A Wise Fellow can be seen exhibiting A Wonderful Follow-through. No Matter when we go to the new school we will find a rambler who is always seeking New Meadows, and in her work is always following the Newest Methods. The sports, too, are in a flourishing condition. The reason why the hockey did so well is that it was conducted by one who is always T.T. As a result of this it has produced Many Large Scores. After a period of inaction of a few sessions the cricket team has been revived, and although our trainer does not profess to be a Jack Hobbs, he has greatly improved our play. After a strenuous Saturday of football or hockey, cricket or netball, we jaded pupils rest our weary limbs at A Kinema entertainment.

All My Work.

And another story Ludus Asinorum, in the same magazine, written by a future English Teacher, Jenny Maxwell, mentions several teachers by name.

Many of the staff were single women- women had to leave employment when they married as seen in 1926 : "Miss Winifred Niven's last day on duty as Infant mistress. She retires on approaching marriage".

One teacher in the 30s and 40s who had quite a reputation for her strictness was:

"Auld **Mag Watson**'s hard to please
Dot your 'I's and stroke your 'T's".

She used to inspect pupils' nails for cleanliness. Boys caught throwing things over the railings outside school were told off by the sarcastic teacher appearing in the playground with a map and telling them to redirect themselves.

She was a smoker who disappeared into the cupboard for a fly smoke. Not that she was the only one. **Mr Williamson**, the technical teacher, (Willie Woodpecker) used to send Ian Nicholson up Townhead Street to Fraser's sweetie shop every Wednesday for, " 20 Gold Flake and a box of matches and have one yourself!" Winston Nelson recalls that the teacher knew the boys were smoking illegally despite them hiding behind

LUDUS ASINORUM.

Some of the teachers, it was rumoured, had been detected secreting shin-guards and football boots in their desks. Accordingly, at four o'clock the Hockey ground was lined by expectant pupils. The game proceeded, and the girls' team played a very good game of HOCKEY. But what could that avail when the teachers were demonstrating to the wondering spectators some strange new game.

We have not been able to procure a copy of the rules of the game, but the reader may get a general idea of it from the following description of the actual play.

Mr Donald, the centre, stood for the greater part of the match beside the goals that the pupils were defending. His task required great skill and nicety of judgment, as it consisted in hitting the ball the second after it had rolled over the sawdust line, to one side or other of the goal posts. On the left wing Miss M'Clennan and Miss Haines stayed so close together or changed places so continually that nobody could tell who was inner and who was wing. Miss Tocher, the right inner, watched intently Mr Donald and Mr Finlayson, who was centre-half, so that she might get in their way whenever they seemed to be going to hit the ball. Miss Skinner, the right wing, ran up and down the field as if she were trying to set up a new record for sprinting, and hit the ball towards the centre of the field whenever she was quite sure that no member of the staff was there. Mr Finlayson usually kicked the ball out of the way of the girls, but now and then, to prove that a stick was really necessary, tried with a full golf swing to send it out of sight. To Mr Whiteley one side of the stick was as good as the other, and if the ball happened to be out of reach, he took careful aim and flung his stick at it. This manœuvre was entirely successful, but we suggest that he should attach his stick to some part of his person by a string, so that it may be the more easily retrieved. The other half-back, Mr Hetherington, was careful to have only one hand on his stick at a time, and to hit the ball not more than once every ten minutes. Miss Hunter, one of the backs, avoided the ball altogether. If it came towards her quickly she eluded it; if slowly, she raised her stick while the rest of the staff held their breath, thinking she was really going to hit it. Mr Mackintosh ran about all over the field, and pushed out of his way, before kicking the ball, any of the opposing team that hampered his progress. When the ball came near Mr Turner, he let his stick fall, caught the ball, and threw it. Perhaps in this game the goal-keeper does not need a stick.

We are sure that this game, a product of the fertile imaginations of the Staff, is destined to become popular, and in that case a name is necessary. We suggest "Ludus Asinorum."

J. K. M. (Class IV.)

The Lockardian 1929

a ditch up at Lambhill, smoking cigarettes then rubbing their nicotine stained fingers on stones to remove the tell tale signs. A blind eye was turned!

Miss Tocher (Tougie) Every former pupil and teacher I spoke to remembered or had heard of this formidable teacher. She taught science and encouraged girls to stay on at school and even appeared at their parents' doors in an attempt to persuade them of the opportunities available. My mother told me that Tougie often went on holiday to Germany in the 1930s and on her return would chastise her pupils with, "Dummkopf, you would really have to sit up and learn if you lived in Germany!" Of course at the time many British people admired Hitler, thinking that he was doing what was best for Germany. Most folk in Scotland had no idea of what was really happening.

A former pupil, John Nicholson, has written some stories centred around this iconic teacher. They are to be found in the appendix.

Miss Nan Little came to teach at Lockerbie when there were still a number of evacuees in the town. When their parents came to collect them, many families decided to remain because they liked the town so much. Nan was in charge of the Girls' Training Corps in Lockerbie, some of whom were still at school.

They were trained to spot aircraft and administer first aid as well as have lessons in astronomy, drill, camping and cookery. Miss Dunlop and Miss Muir assisted Miss Little, but not when she took 20 young women to London on her own for a parade. She supervised them without a hitch; got them back on the sleeper to Lockerbie, arriving at 6 am and, whilst the girls went home and slept off their excitement, she had to turn up at school a couple of hours later to continue teaching. Mr Hetherington could not do to have her off another day!

In keeping with the times Miss Little left her teaching post when she married. Her GTC gave her a wonderful send off.

Girls Training Corps outside the Academy
In middle of front row are the organisers Miss Muir, Miss Little and Miss Dunlop.
The author's mother is in the back row far right.

Wedding Photo of Nan Little (Geography teacher and officer of GTC) to Captain Worton. Sanquhar 1949 includes Mary and Blanche Graham.

Her father (J E Little) had also been a teacher at Lockerbie and taught a P7 class during the First World War when Mr Malcolm was rector.

Mr Little had been a head teacher at Ewes Primary School at the tender age of 23!

Mrs Ada Fraser (Lemonada) was the lady supervisor in the 1960s. Her role was rather like that of a guidance teacher. Checking hemlines and dispensing aspirin to girls, she also taught English and Latin.

Pupils in the 1960s and 70s will remember Arthur Johnstone who taught English. Many particularly enjoyed his Friday afternoon lessons when he brought out his guitar and sang to the class. Arthur is quite an archivist. I discovered that he has even kept his old mark books! He was keen on football and helped coach the teams.

Another of Arthur's claims to fame was his TV appearance on "Sale of the Century" which generated much excitement amongst his pupils.

Ian Caplan taught French and scared the living daylights out of us wee first years. He looked a bit like Bela Lugosi with his sleek black hair and black gown. He used to point to marks on the wall and say that these were former pupils!

Harry Reid recalls taking over as PE teacher from the janitor in 1952. If that was unusual then even more so was when he first started teaching at Gretna he had replaced the Queen of the South goalkeeper!

Paperwork comes to PE

Here is Harry in his office snowed under with paperwork. He was soon to be summoned to take his place in the front row for a school staff photo. He had time to change out of his sports' gear, except for his footwear. A point that he was chastised for by Ada Fraser when she saw the photo (staff photo 1962).

Matt Green taught History in the 1960s. Ian Forbes remembers being told by him that "Hell will freeze over before you get your history O grade ", but he did! He is also remembered for his badminton playing and for using the racquet in class to poke answers out of reluctant pupils. An MG midget, fake tan and coal black (dyed) hair were his trademarks. I still remember the Duke of Marlborough's "telephone number"- BROM 4689 the dates and names of his victories in the 17th Century War of the Spanish Succession thanks to Matt.

Back Row L-R: Niall Wetherstone, Peter Porteous, Dave Wilson. Front: Ian Forbes, Kenny Anderson, Dougie Cameron

David TR Wilson. In the 1970s Mr Wilson was universally welcomed - a young teacher with a refreshingly modern style - sitting on a desk - not behind it - and letting us discuss the issues of the day, respecting our sometimes naive political views. He also played guitar with some senior boys in a group called The Full Circle.

Jan Ritchie. Jan was another young teacher who was very popular at school, giving up a lot of her time training choirs for school and County events. She later became an HMI.

Choir 1966/7 trained by Jan Ritchie
Back Row L-R: Yvonne Cameron, 2, Anne -, 4, Janetta Robb, Linda Herrick, Jean Houston, Ann Bland, 9, Miss Ritchie, Vera Armstrong
Middle Row L-R: Rosemary Gibson, Lynna Baxter, Anne Morton, Anne Wells, Valerie Martin,
Karen Currie, Una Irving, Carole Nutt, Elizabeth Mitchell, Rosemary Carruthers
Front Row L-R: Eileen Bell, Nancy Mackie, Linda Murray, 4, 5, Stuart McQueen, David Paisley, Allyson Reid, Lynne Johnstone, 10, James Twidale

Some of year V1 in 1990
Teachers: Tom Russell and Phil Quinn, Jillian Bell,
Graham Weatherup, Jennifer Newman, Alison Hinselwood,
Douglas Brown, Paul Weatherup, Sally Graham.

Tom Russell. Tom taught Geography. In his first week at Lockerbie Academy in 1969 he was asked in the main staff room by Arthur Johnstone where the Cayman Islands were as it was a clue for his crossword. He hazarded a guess - the Indian Ocean - only to discover that they were in the West Indies! He was never allowed to forget that and at his retiral he was presented with a map of Central America with the Cayman Islands highlighted.

Douglas Lipton, poet, was born in 1953 in Glasgow, but taught at the Academy. He started writing poetry in his teens. In collaboration with Kevin McIntrye and Karen Wimhurst he

```
Lockerbie   Academy   Top   30   Hits

1.   Three Steps to Heaven          Praying Pottie
2.   Needles and Pins               Pat and the Popkins
3.   Walk Tall                      Howlin' Harvie
4.   All the Nice Girls love a sailor  H. M. S. Suspence
5.   Funky Moped                    The Yellow Peril  (Room 10)
6.   Lost in France                 Travelling Thomson
7.   Flower of Scotland             Flora McDonald
8.   Art for Art's Sake             Swingin' Little and the Chess Men
9.   Rockin' all over the World     Russell 'n' Buckle
10.  Hot Legs                       Freezing Fiona and the Physically Fit
11.  Roll over Lay down             Ada and the Disprins
12.  The Northern Lights of Old Aberdeen  Ambling Alex
13.  Money, Money, Money            Pound and the Blue Notes
14.  I do, I do, I do, I do, I do   Weatherstone and the Wedlocks
15.  Bitter Fingers                 Agnes Rallentando and the Augmentations
16.  If it Wasnae fur yer wellies   Mucker McEwan
17.  Football Crazy                 Brycey and the Penalties
18.  If I had Words                 Arthur and the Adjectives
19.  Why Did it Have to Be Me       Miss Dither  (Room 12)
20.  I'd like to teach the World to Sing  Wolfgang Adrian Mozart
21.  On the Blue Ridge Mountains of Virginia  Dr. on Horseback
23.  A Gordon for Me                McNay's Little Lady
24.  Daddy Cool                     Papa Jeff
25.  Oxygene                        Craig and the Crickets
26.  Don't Cry for Me Hightae       Rockin' Robson
27.  Home, Home On the Range        Saucy Sandra
28.  Ma Baker                       The Welsh Female Voice Choir
29.  Jack In The Box                Groovy Geckie
30.  Here Comes The Sun             Happy Halliday

PUPIL QUOTE - "IS YOUR JACKET REAL LEATHER OR IS IT JUST
          SYMPATHETIC ?" !!       19
```

A guess the teacher quiz from 1978

wrote the libretto for **Songs for a Falling Angel** which is a requiem for Lockerbie. At the 1995 dedication ceremony in Arlington Cemetery two of Douglas' poems were read by the family of one of the victims of Pan Am Flight 103.

Janitors

Janitors 1990
Andy Anderson and Jimmy Viviers

Unusually in 1873 a woman was employed to light fires and clean the school rooms.

In 1889, the janitor was **Adam Bunch**, an ex-drum major of the Black Watch who had fought in the Ashanti War. He was also in charge of military drill.

In the 1930s a janitor named **Mr Starkey** is remembered for having a belt and using it! Whether or not he actually had the authority to mete out this type of punishment is debateable.

In the 1940s **Sergeant Kirkwood** was the janitor and, like Adam Bunch, was also in charge of Physical Education.

Mr John Beck, Mr James Sloan and **Mr James Viviers** covered the 1970s, 80s and 90s. **Mr Robert Kerr** is the present Head Janitor and has 3 assistants.

Secretarial Staff

The first official **School Secretary** was Scotty - **Eileen Scott**.

In 1942 Eileen one day was a pupil and the next was the secretary. She remained secretary until 1990. She told me that even when in employment she could not be on first name terms with the teachers and still had to follow the school rules such as keeping to the left when walking the corridors.

L-R Mrs I Sutton, Mrs L Lamb, Mrs J Hawkins, (Mr J Vivers),
Miss S. Marshall, Mrs K. Dougan, Mrs E Scott

One of her first tasks was to check the inventory for war supplies - the blankets and gas masks. Her other jobs were collecting money from pupils for National Savings and dinner money; weighing the rosehips collected by the children and matching the pupils to the farmers for tattie picking work.

The computerisation of records, registration and attendance; the proliferation of paperwork including correspondence with various agencies; statistics for the Council, Scottish Qualifications Authority and Parliament; forms, school reports, letters to parents, newsletters, prospectus etc now require 6 office staff. One of the longest standing members of the secretarial staff was **Sandra Marshall**. Sandra was another pupil who came to work in the school office. She stayed 35 years. She also taught typing, and later, computing at evening class.

Lockerbie Academy Primary Staff 1960
Isabel Tait, 2, Ruby Reid, 4, Mrs Gordon, Meg Roberts,
Cathie Mackie (Head), Audrey Irving, 9, Marion Armstrong

Librarians

Ruby Reid was the first official **School Librarian** although a library had been established as early as 1901.

Ruby had been teaching music and providing cover for absent teachers. In Lochmaben she was called **Ruby Tuesday** because that was her day there. She was interested in developing the library and to her husband encouraged her to apply for the job when it was formally advertised.

School Library

Pupils who wanted to avoid being outdoors in break time in the winter queued up to be Library Monitors. Now the library, as well as being in a different location, looks quite different.

The present Librarian is **Mrs Langlands** and one of her jobs is to oversee the use of the computers. Pupils can use these to search the internet and do homework during lunchtime.

Catering

In October 1944 Education committee meals were prepared at Dornock and the helpers were **Miss McRobert** and **Mrs Kerr** who served the pupils 210 2-course meals. **Mrs Henderson**, the school cook and her assistant **Miss Bell** left in November 1944 three days before the final decision was made to opt for the Dornock meals which had been trialled for 3 weeks. This implies that they were no longer needed. Were they sacked, made redundant or did they leave in a stushie?

The present "Catering Manager" is **Karen Beck**.

Dinner Ladies 1990
R-L: Fiona Robertson, Fiona -, Karen Beck

When Karen was a pupil at the school the pots of hot dinners were served to each table by kitchen staff. One pupil from each table was responsible for dishing up the meal for the others; collecting the plates and cutlery and taking them to the counters.

Since she started in the kitchens in 1983 she has seen huge changes in the school dinner system. The cafeteria system in particular has changed the way of eating at school. The menu offers plenty of healthy choices from hot or cold meals, sandwiches and rolls and now there are no fizzy drinks or chocolate in the vending machines. The room is designed to look like a cafe and older pupils are happy to spend time

School Cafeteria

there chatting and relaxing on their "free" periods. as well as listening to the radio system run by pupils for pupils called LA2day.

It was quite a different story over 100 years ago. On the 11th of February 1887 the headmaster recorded that :" On Tuesday several ladies inaugurated dinners for children from the country which have proved a great success". This was long before the School Meals Act, but children were travelling long distances from home to school and needed hot food. In 1911: "Hot soup has been supplied to the pupils who want it at a charge of half a penny this week. About 230 pupils have taken advantage of the arrangements daily".

In the 1930s Mrs Kirkwood ran the kitchen where pupils could buy broth and a roll for a few pennies. Some pupils went down to the station to get hot tea and in the 1960s we used to go down to de Luca's cafe to buy hot Vimto.

Travel

Travel to and from school was by bus in the 20th century. Greens used to run many of the buses and some older former pupils will remember my maternal grandfather, **Hector Shennan**, who drove the Caledonian school buses in the 1930s.

Other Staff

The present staff include auxiliaries, technicians, home-link and community learning workers as well as support for learning assistants and behaviour support staff.

*Hector Shennan
-the author's maternal grandfather who drove the school bus in the 30s.*

The Senior Management Team 2006

*Mr G G Ferrie
Depute Rector (Senior)
Head of Milk House*

*Mrs S M Bain
Depute Rector
Head of Kirtle House*

*Mr S J Cotter
Depute Rector
Head of Dryfe House*

*Mrs B Lewis
Depute Rector*

*Mrs D Reid
School Support Manager*

Staff Photos

Staff c1923-6
Back Row L-R: Miss Black, Mr Finlayson, Mr Whiteley, Mr Hetherington, Miss Tocher
2nd Row: Miss Richardson, Miss Horne, Mr Donald, Miss Watson, Dr -, Miss Maclennan, ?
3rd Row: Mr Welsh, Miss Rioch, Headmaster Mr Muir Burns, Miss Hunter, Mr Turner, Miss Carutthers
Front Row: Miss Skinner, Miss McDonnell.

Staff 1946/7
Back Row L-R: Betty MacLean (Dom Sc), Bill Williamson (Woodwork), 3, Sgt Kirkwood (PE),
"Daddy" Ross (Geog, Hist, Eng), Flora Muir (Dom Sc)
Middle Row L-R: Ada Fraser (Latin), Miss Dunlop (p7), Miss Black, Miss Little (Geog, His), Mr Inglis (Music),
Miss Clark (French), Mrs McGuffog (Z class), Mag Watson, at side Eileen Scott (sec)
Front Row L-R: 1, Miss Sandilands (P), Miss McConnel (Infants), Mr Hetherington (HT), Miss Tocher (Sci),
Miss Carruthers (Sewing), Mrs Hetherington.

Staff 1949
Back Row L-R: R Creighton (Art), Mr Kerr (Maths), Mr Inglis (Music), Mr Williamson (Technical),
Mr Richmond, Mr Hendry (French), JDS Martin (Science), Mr Roan
Middle Row: Sgt Kirkwood (PE), Eileen Scott (Secretary), Moya Elliot, Mrs J Moffat, Miss M Wilson, Mr Gordon (English),
Kate Swan, Hazel Oliver, Elspeth Currie, Miss Stewart (History) Miss Goldie
Front Row: Miss Gordon (Mrs A Fraser), Miss Park, Mrs Hetherington, Miss Currie, Mr Hetherington (Headmaster),
Miss Tocher (Science) Mrs McGuffog (Slow learners), Miss K Mackie, Miss Richardson.

Staff 1952
Back Row L-R: Bob Creighton (glasses), Harry Reid, Cowboy Kerr
Second Row L-R: 1 Mr Gungston, Josh Martin, Mr Blacklaws, Mr Ross, Mr Cunningham
Third Row L-R: Mrs Robertson, Miss Richardson, Eileen Scott, Margaret Condie, Sheena Beattie, Mrs Murray, 7
Fourth Row L-R: Miss Richardson, Jenny Maxwell, Cath Mackie, Hazel Oliver,
Jean Richardson, 6, Miss Stewart, Mrs Currie, Mrs McGuffog, Kate Swan
Front Row L-R: Isobel Pointon, Miss Coupland, Mrs Hetherington, Mr Gordon,
Mr Hetherington, Miss Tocher, Miss Currie, Bob Williamson, Mag Watson

Staff 1962

Back Row L-R: Audrie Irving, Yvonne Callendar, Dorothy Adamson, Jen Wilson, Sheila Hill, Connie Wilson, Nellie Brown, Isobel Tait, Ian Robson, Cambell Brown,Josh Martin, Joyce Robson, George Hood, Davie Ferguson, Ian McKenzie, Mrs Johnstone, Dolly Gordon
Middle Row L-R: Mrs Hetherington, Marjorie Smith, Marion Armstrong, Greta Rankine, French student,
Mrs Miller, Jan Ritchie, Mrs Jessiman, Jim Sloan, Ken Michie, Leslie Cunningham, Archie Morton, Jenny Maxwell,
Jim Maltman, Dixie Ingram, Peter Bourne, Marion Armstrong, Hazel Scott, Mrs Meg Roberts,
Front Row L-R: Jack Geekie, Ian Caplan, Liz Briggs, Margaret Ward, Reg Creighton, Harry Reid, George Gronbach, Mat Miller,
AJ Simpson, Mrs Simpson,Ada Fraser, Cath Mackie, George Tait, Alan Welsh, Matt Green, Eric Williams.

Staff 1975

Back Row L-R: - Younger, G Oswald, G Weatherstone, R Steadman, L Buckle, G McCallion, C Gardiner,S McPherson,
I McNeil, F Murphy, A Jackson, J Mitchell, A Douglas, J Halliday, S J Brown, Rev. D Pottie
2nd Back Row: J Cartwright, D Adamson, J Moffat,S Gilchrist,E Miller, E Taylor, J Roddick, A Johnstone,
G Fraser, G Spence, J McGonigal, J Roberts, L Spence, D Rae, K Waddell, M Crawford
2nd Front Row: J Moffat, I Wyllie, A Warden, Mrs Kelly, A Morburn, (Cobbett), C Wilson, P Baird,
W Bryce, J Geekie, G Hood, W Little, J Rae, D Wilson, G Macrae, A Tough, N McBride, 18, 19,
E Brown, A McGarrie, P Cairns, L Young, L Herrick, C Cunningham
Front Row: G Rankin, D Chisholm, A Irving, W McTaggart, P Welsh, C Brown, J Geekie, R Creighton, A Welsh, Rector,
W Anderson, G Gronbach, A Fraser, H Reid, W Thomson, J Gair, T Russell, M Armstrong, R McEwan, I Robson.

The Staff of 1978 "Renoir Style" from the "MOSAIC"

Staff 1990

Back Row (6th) L-R: Keith Milar, Dereck Brockett, Bill McTaggart, Lindsay Buckle, Tim Birrell, Raymond Henry, Keith McCord, David Hughes, Alan Cairns, Tom Lindsay.
(5th): Mike Williams, John Roddick, Ken Wilkie, Alastair Gordon, Hugh Young, Phil Quinn, Gordon McNay, Peter Kirk, Dave Pound, Jim Rae, Irene Sutton
(4th): Jean Gordon, Wilma Thomson, Robin Kerr, Denis Chisholm, Steve Robinson, Mal McCrudden, Listy Aeons, Ken Gordon, Andy Morton, Claire Murphy
(3rd): Fiona McColl, Anne Strachan, Paul Jardine, Julie Mills, Fiona Dunlop, Gordon McKie, Greg Oswald, Alison McGarrie, Janet Rogerson, Joyce McGarrie
(2nd): Mary Rankin, Helen Wright, Pam Farrell, Grace McBain, Evelyn Miller, Strona Petty, Jean Morton, Pam Baird, Barbara Lewis,
Sheena Burgess, Sheila Briggs, Liz Stewart, Maureen Reid, Lorna Lamb
Front Row: Dot Young, Arthur Johnstone, Bill Dalrymple, Graham Myle, Pat Cairns, Rector, Drew Blake, Gordon Ferrie, Dave Wilson, Janice Haskins, Joe Boardman, Colin McTaggart.

Curriculum

In 1893 the Minutes of the School Board stipulated that instruction be given in the Bible and catechism and that there would be a committee set up to monitor this. By then the church had lost its control over education, but its influence was to remain.

Until 1891 schooling was not free. In the 1873 Minutes of the School Board a scale of fees was set down: 9d per month for Infants ranging to 1/2d for Standards V and VI. Four or more higher branches (subjects) cost 3/6d. The higher branches were Latin, French, Greek, German, Mathematics, Navigation, Book Keeping and Drawing. In the winter months parents were also expected to pay for coals as well as ink pens and pen holders.

The following extracts from the school log books illustrate the changing curriculum:-

In 1875 Mr Thomson who was covering for Mr Muir during his sickness: "Found children backwards and deficient especially in arithmetic," but Inspector Barrie's* report in October commended the Mixed School, "In all departments of this large school, the results of the year's work are very creditable to the zeal of the teachers." This might have been partly because the headmaster had made some changes, for example alterations in the time table substituting Physiology for German.

For reading Nelson's Royal Readers were purchased and in 1881 a new headmaster, Mr Palmer, 10 days into his headship, "Commenced 10 boys in Latin and 5 in bookkeeping."

A mention is made of history and geography courses on 4th April 1884: "History - James 11 then Anne's reign; Geography - lakes and 8 countries."

In Nov 1887:
"Gave orders for pupils to supply themselves with the books necessary for their new classes. One change in books only has been made viz. instead of Collins' Geography and History - that of Chambers' has been introduced."

4th April 1890:
"First cookery lesson today. 48 girls from Standard V and V1 and Ex V1 attended 2 hours demonstration in the forenoon and 24 girls of the V1 and Ex V1 Standards were selected for practice in the afternoon." Boys were not allowed to attend cookery classes and girls, woodwork or technical, until the passing of the Sex Discrimination Act in 1975.

6th Oct 1890:
"Standards V1 and Ex V1 were examined orally on the Geography of Africa."

1892 :
"Pupil teachers of 4th year examined in History 1066-1509". (Important English History dates - Norman Conquest to Henry V111. What happened to Scottish History?)

Dec 23rd 1896:
"School dismissed afternoon - the infants were given an hour's entertainment with Fairy Tales."

The HMI report of this year gives an indication of the subjects taught at this time:

* Relative of writer JM Barrie, author of **Peter Pan**.

"Ably conducted by Mr Malcolm and his most competent staff...a creditable amount of work in Higher English, Latin, Greek, French and German and Agriculture. Domestic Economy and Shorthand also deserve high commendation."

In 1901 the school was commended as the seniors were reading: "Very difficult French authors".

A new kitchen for the cookery classes was built in 1896 and the following year woodwork was introduced. Practical skills were badly needed especially for pupils who would be going out to work at the age of 13.

A rare treat would have been the advent of the Gramophone to Lockerbie on August 8th 1898. This wonderful invention was brought into school by "Chief Engineer, Johnstone" and the pupils were able to hear "every sound distinctly" of 'Killarney' and 'Scots whae Hae'. Nowadays, CDs, ipods and MP3 players are everywhere.

(Earlier that year the pupils and townsfolk were able to go to the cinema for the first time. Pictures were shown of Queen Victoria's diamond jubilee; a snowball fight and scenes from Paris and New York. They had, however, to wait a long time for the Rex Cinema to open - luxuriously furnished; thrice weekly showings for up to 800 folk, in July 1933).

NB 1897 and 1898 were years for firsts for Lockerbie folk. The children would have been amazed when the first motor car appeared in Lockerbie in September 1897, drawing a large crowd of spectators. It was noted that later in the year: "Another car passed through, having done 46 miles in four and a half hours."

Visitors often came to the school to give talks. The Scottish Band of Hope wished to lecture on the use and abuse of alcohol in 1897 and on September 22nd 1899: "Standard V1 taken with Lantern for **Pied Piper of Hamelin**." ie Lantern Slides.

On the 6th June 1900 the seniors were treated to a first hand account: "Of the current preoccupation of the Boer War, Mr Frank Wightman, from Kimberley, visited the school and gave an account of his experiences as one of the besieged townsmen. Mr Wightman's story was substituted for the ordinary Geography lesson...the scholars were much interested".

A list of teachers' hours from the Minutes of the school board indicates the variety of subjects taught by the teachers (Multi - tasking).

Mr Cameron taught 3 hours of English Literature; 2 hours each of History and Geography; 6 hours of French; 3 hours of Shorthand ; 2 hours of Singing and 12 hours of Latin. Mr McLemont taught 3 hours of English Literature; 4 hours each of History, Geography and French; 3 hours of Bookkeeping; 6 hours each of Drawing and Latin.

The headmaster also taught 3 hours of English Literature and 5 hours of French. Very seldom do head teachers take classes now as they are expected to work as managers. In 1903 there were attempts to make teachers responsible for one subject only, but nowadays teachers are again being encouraged to train to teach a variety of subjects to make them more employable as it makes staffing and time tabling easier.

By 1901 the chairman brought up the question of the better teaching of manners in the school generally and submitted the rules of 'The Children's National Guild of Courtesy'. The subject was cordially received by the Board and it was agreed that the matter should be continued till the September meeting.

In 1904 the Glasgow and Annandale Association called alleging that the history text book was written from an English point of view and: "Seriously misrepresents the history of Scotland." The board wrote to them to ask them to list the inaccuracies. It turned out that the main problem was the use of the word "England" for Britain.

Also in 1904 experimental science was introduced and there was a proposal for a school orchestra. In the same year a Drawing Teacher from Carlisle was appointed to teach on Fridays and get her train fares paid.

The following year there is a mention of a school prospectus - not such a modern idea after all - and the use of native French teachers.

War with Germany was declared in 1914 and people were becoming more patriotic. The chairman of the school board stated that the headmaster required: "A further supply of lead pencils for use in the school which had hitherto been obtained from Messrs Fabre in Bavaria. " In view of the war it was agreed that these pencils should in future be obtained from British manufacturers.

In the same year the board approached Mr Malcolm suggesting a change in the curriculum in the scheme of needlework: "To allow the pupils to substitute the knitting of socks and making of shirts in place of pinafores, night-dresses etc. as the former will be of more use to the troops in service". These are more examples of how controlling of the currilum the School Board could be.

In the 1930s pupils remember that every day began with registration and a hymn. Up until the Qualifying exam at age 11, the subjects were Arithmetic, English, History and Geography, with Art and Music taught in the wooden shed.

Afterwards Science, Algebra, Geometry, French and Latin were introduced.

In Geography the first study was of the county of Dumfries; then rivers and mountains, the British Isles and the British Empire and some work was done on Europe.

History was English History (still Henry VIII). Nothing was taught about the First World War probably because it was too fresh in folks' memories, but the pupils were taught about the Boer War. Pupils were not taken on day trips possibly because of the poor financial climate.

In the late 30s Miss Hunter who taught History began the session with:

> "Geography is the story of man's environment and History is the story of man's achievements."

There was little recognition of ordinary folks' history and far less of women's roles in History.

In 1945 when Miss Little came to teach Geography and History at Lockerbie Academy her inspiration was this teacher, Miss "Puff" Hunter, but she didn't follow her teaching methods. She recalls that her style of teaching was not usual at the time - but in fact it is now the widely used technique of allowing the pupils to find out for themselves rather than be taught unquestioningly by rote.

In 1944 Gardening was an important subject because of wartime rationing. The school garden had been considerably extended since the war began and was cultivated by boys in the non-language classes. Potatoes and common garden vegetables were grown and the HMI suggested that the area be increased "as a valuable food supply". Under the ASDAN awards scheme gardening has been reintroduced and Ms Rogerson, the teacher in charge, is building a greenhouse from recycled plastic bottles!

In the 1960s former pupil, George Porteous, took the opportunity from age 13 to attend the Barony College of Agriculture. There he received a school education as well as lessons on milking cows, animal and crop husbandry and fitting engines.

The Barony was run like a barracks with similar punishments for misdeeds. Peeing in other boys' wellies meant loss of privileges.

This school was residential, and free for inhabitants of Dumfriesshire. Boys from outwith the county had to pay, but many did come from as far afield as Birmingham and Glasgow.

At Lockerbie the opportunity to learn Ancient Greek was offered to Latin scholars by Mr Campbell Brown in the 1960s although very few took up the option. Nowadays there are hardly any state schools offering even Latin.

In the Third Statistical Account (1962) the Rev Steen records: "Latin, French and experimental science are taught, but the school stresses the practical side with gardening, domestic science and dressmaking, woodwork and similar studies. The English 'house system' has been introduced and sports and field games have grown more important."

Drama and Music have always been popular both in school and as exra-curricular activities. School choirs, in particular, have featured greatly in the prize lists of Dumfries Music Festivals and plays are annually presented by the school at Christmas time.

Drama 1988 - The King and I
Back Row L-R: Sarah, Kirsteen, Tessa, Frazer, Fiona, Helen, Roy, Jethro, Frances, Cathyrn, Tracey
Front Row L-R: Victoria, Colin, Raymond, 4, 5

RAYMOND PATTIE S6 1992

"Grease" is the fourth school show in which I've been involved. I have always had a strong interest in drama and was given my first opportunity to take part when, in 1988, I was the Crown Prince Chululongkorn in the "King and I". Later that same year I played "Scrooge", the miserable Dickens character which I really enjoyed performing.

In 1989 I was cast as the Scarecrow in the "Wizard of Oz", a show which I remember being great fun to rehearse and perform. In "Grease" I play Teen Angel who advises beauty school dropout Frenchy to return to Rydell High.

Sadly this will be my last chance to be in the annual production before I leave Lockerbie Academy to go to Art College in the autumn. I'm really looking forward to meeting new people, progressing my drawing and painting further.

Everyone works hard to maintain the high standards set each year in the school show. I personally feel that taking part has been an enjoyable and worthwhile experience and I hope they continue to be as successful in the future.

Raymond Pattie

page 9

JOSHUA LONG S6 1992

"Grease" is the first school show that I've taken part in and "Kenickie" is my first big acting role! After the summer holidays I start a one year foundation course at Cumbria College of Art and from there I'll hopefully progress to do Design/Graphic Design at Dundee College of Art.

LYNSEY BROWN S6 1992

I leave Lockerbie Academy this summer after an eventful and enjoyable six years. I have been involved in all the school shows since I came to Lockerbie Academy and am now going on to Drama College to further my career. I have been accepted on a one year foundation course at Fife Drama College and possibly the Royal Scottish Academy of Music and Drama. This is a three year degree course. If I am not accepted this year I shall try again until I am!!

Hopefully at the end of the degree course I will be qualified and good enough to find work as a drama teacher.

All this would not have been possible without the help, encouragement and support of the staff and pupils at Lockerbie Academy and of course my family and friends.

Joshua Long

Lynsey Brown

page 10

*Part of Programme for Grease
with the principal players*

Poster for LA production of Grease 1992

*The Elastic Band 1977
Caroline Smith, Victoria Beveridge, Linda Wolff, Margaret McBride
formed the LA Folk group in 1974*

The curriculum in 2007 is very different.

In S1 and S2 pupils follow a common course, studying either French or German. This course includes English, Maths, Social Subjects (History, Geography and Modern Studies), Science, PE, Home Economics, Art, Music, RE, PSE (Personal and Social Education),Technical Education, Drama and ICT (Information and Computing Technology).

By S3 and S4 pupils begin to specialise as they consider their future careers. This leads to national examinations. Further specialisation takes place after S4.The century old Higher examination still exists, but in a completely unrecognisable form. Pupils can study at different levels according to their ability and age- Access, Intermediate, Higher and Advanced Higher. Standard grades have replaced "O" grades, but they themselves are soon likely to disappear.

A large percentage of youngsters now stay on for a 5th and 6th year and provision is made for work experience. Subjects such as enterprise education and life skills are also included in the curriculum.

Around 60% of the leavers go onto either further or higher education.

Teaching styles have also changed. Pupils are much more encouraged to speak a foreign language rather than only read and write it although there were visiting native French teachers as early as 1905. "They were given paid board and lodgings" presumably to coax reluctant students as well as extend their own English knowledge.

Recently some criticism have been made about the "dumbing down" of the curriculum, but perhaps what has changed is the focus. Teachers are now facilitators; pupils are allowed to question and research for themselves. The emphasis is on where and how to access information.

There is no longer a separate Arithmetic national examination paper, but readers may like to try some of these arithmetical problems. Note that a certain amount of literary ability is also required.

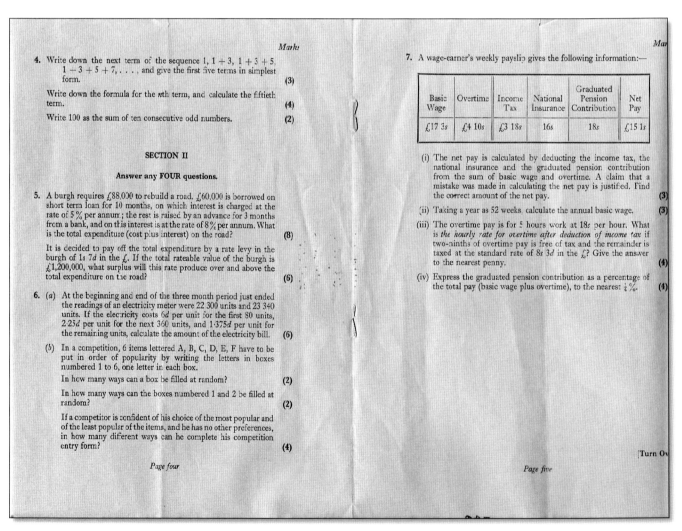

Selected pages from O grade Arithmetic Exam paper 1969

Former Pupils

Some former Lockerbie Academy pupils have achieved fame; some have made huge differences to other people' lives at home and abroad, but many have stayed in the district contributing to the local community, keeping long established businesses and farms alive. Sadly some have been tragically cut down in their youth.

Scots have always been well travelled folk; keen to explore or settle in new lands. Lockerbie Academy pupils are no different. Here, in no particular order, I have highlighted just a few of the academy's former pupils to illustrate the range of their achievements.

Phil Sanderson

In 2006 Phil and his wife, Pauline, became the first married couple from the UK to climb to the top of Mt Everest. They both work at Glenmore Lodge Outdoor Centre near Aviemore.

Lorna Young 1952-1996

Lorna attended the Academy from 1968-1970 to spend her 5th and 6th years after Langholm Academy. Lorna was a striking red headed student with a mind of her own. She worked in the publishing trade in Edinburgh, but later found more fulfilling work with Equal Exchange - an organisation which promotes Fair Trade. Soon afterwards she split her working week so that she could work with the newly formed Cafe Direct. This was another FairTrade company which concentrated on Coffee.

Lorna became Sales Director and was the person who persuaded Scotmid and Safeways to initially stock this coffee. This was hard work and required dedication and strong persuasive skills as many store managers did not understand the principles of Fair Trade. Just before her untimely death in 1996, Lorna was in the throes of negotiating with Sainsburys.

She would have been truly amazed that her work meant that farmers in Central America were benefiting from her pioneering, single-mindedness and forthright persuasiveness. Cafe Direct is now a household name and Scotland is proposing to become a Fair Trade nation. The Lorna Young Foundation now exists to help finance farmers in countries in Central America and Africa to establish their own businesses and make a decent standard of living for their families.

William Maxwell 1912-1998

William was born at 16 Douglas Terrace Lockerbie. He was the only son of Isabella Johnstone Maxwell nee Burnie and James Maxwell who was the grocer and wine and spirit merchant. His grandfather was also a wine merchant of Victoria Square.

William was awarded a first prize in English History and French in 1927 when he was in Class 1VH.G. He was awarded the William Sanders Gold Medal for the session 1927-28 when he gained his Higher Education Leaving Certificate in English, Literature, History Mathematics, Latin, French and Science.

He went to Edinburgh University to study medicine. After graduation he worked in Scotland and England as a surgeon before the war. He was posted to Norway after joining the RAMC and after the war he worked in India and Burma. He was awarded the honorary rank of Major and he became a GP in England until his retiral in 1982.

Anne Rafferty (see class photo 1945)

Anne attended both primary and secondary schools in Lockerbie becoming Dux in 1947. She continued her studies at Dumfries Academy and then Edinburgh University where she studied Law and History. Anne worked as a solicitor with the firm McJerrow and Stevenson from 1955 to 2007.

She has contributed much to local life : she was instrumental in raising funds for and establishing the Little Theatre; she served as a director of Scottish Enterprise for Dumfries and Galloway and has campaigned for the MacMillan and Cancer Relief Funds. For her services to business she was awarded a MBE in 1997.

Maitland Pollock

Maitland gained fame in the neighbourhood when he was spotted as a potential professional footballer while attending Lockerbie Academy in the 1960s. He played for Nottingham Forrest as well as Luton and Queen of the South.

James Boyd 1891-1970

James was born in 1891, the only son of Peter Boyd, master blacksmith of Gardiner's Close. Whilst at Lockerbie, he won the Athenaeum Open Scholarship in Music in1909.

He trained as a violinist in Glasgow and Berlin where he met his future wife Anna Maria Smulders. He became a soloist in Tchaikovsky's Violin Concerto with the Hamburg Orchestra in 1911 and 1912.

Unfortunately war broke out in 1914 and James (with the Durham Light Infantry) was wounded at the battle of the Somme in 1916. The nerve of his right arm was completely severed. This put an end to his violinist career. He had to rebuild his life.

As he had spent 4 years in Germany he decided to study German. He went to Oxford University and graduated with a first class degree and took a Ph.D at Heidelberg. He worked in S Africa and later became Taylor Professor of German in 1938.

He worked with Sir Basil Blackwell on the development of some forty editions of German authors and works for use in British Universities and schools.

He always remained active in musical circles and proud of his Scottish roots.

Much of this account was given by his great niece, Jan Church, and comes from the introduction to The Era of Goethe, a Collection of Essays presented to James on his retirement in 1959. The photo is the frontispiece from this book.

Pearl Gaitskill nee Lindsay

Pearl attended the school in the early 1980s

She now works for a charity organisation looking after HIV+/AIDS children in South Africa. She is very thankful for her German lessons at school which has formed the basis for her fluency in Afrikaans!

Sir David Knox

attended Lockerbie Academy from 1938-48 before moving to Dumfries Academy. He studied at Heriot-Watt University as well as in London. He became Vice Chairman of the Conservative Party in 1974-5.

Martin Oliver was elected to the Scottish Parliament in 1999 for Livingston as a Scottish Liberal Democrat MSP.

Stephen Sword b 1980

Won the British Motocross championship in every class in 2000.

Alison Munro b 1954 (See photo 1969 Girlsa 3AC)

Alison, from Lochmaben, was featured in a TV documentary about the making of the "Morse" series. Alison was the wardrobe mistress.

David Mundell now Conservative MP for the region, was a former head boy. He contributed a short poem to the School Magazine, "The Mosaic" in 1976.

Bill Howatson

Billy, from Templand, attended Lochmaben Primary School and then Lockerbie Academy from 1965-71. He became a journalist writing for **The Scottish Farmer** and then for the **Aberdeen Press and Journal** as its agricultural editor. He has won several press awards. He was elected as a Liberal Democrat councillor in 1999 and in 2007 has become the Civil Provost of Aberdeenshire.

Bill Howatson with the author and her dog c1966

Robert Black

He attended Lockerbie and Dumfries Academies before studying law. Professor Black is well known for his involvement in the establishment of the court at Zeiss in Holland for the trial of Abdull Al Megrahi.

Alison Fell

Alison came to Dumfriesshire when she was a little girl and attended Lochmaben Primary, Lockerbie Academy where she was Dux in 1959 and then went to Dumfries. Alison was involved in one of the first Women's Liberation groups; worked on the radical newspaper, **Ink** and **Spare Rib** magazine and has since published novels and poems.

Erin McLaughlin

Was a Syracuse scholar in 2003, but decided to continue her University education there. She graduated in 2007 in History, but also was awarded the honour of being one of two class Marshalls. This award is given for academic achievement, involvement in student organisations and campus and community services.

Hazel Armstrong

Hazel spent her primary schooling in Ecclefechan, before transferring to Lockerbie for her secondary education. After attending university she became a Librarian in the House of Commons.

Susan Rhind

Susan, of Lochmaben, has just been appointed Professor of Veterinary Medicine and Education at Edinburgh.(2007)

Andrew McAllister

Andrew is a painter and musician, born in Lauder in 1959 and educated at Lockerbie Academy. As well as painting he plays acoustic guitar and has been supported by the Royal London Philharmonic Orchestra.

Renwick MacArthur

Renwick MacArthur was born in Lockerbie in 1923. He learned to play several musical instruments including the fiddle and after the war was treasurer of Lockerbie British Legion Pipe Band. As well as working as a construction planning engineer, he has toured and played the fiddle around the world. He has composed music for the fiddle and accordian some of which refer to his birthplace and childhood friends: the "Mid Annandale Comrades", "The Lass Frae Lochmaben" and "Well Street Weans". These compositions can be found in "The Dryfesdale Collection."

Nick De Luca

The 24 year old is making his mark on the rugby pitch. He plays centre for the Scotland A squad. In 2007 his star is shining.

Erin being 'capped' by the Chancellor of Syracuse University

One of the many display cabinets

Gifts and Prizes

Over the years the school has been presented with a number of unusual gifts.

A Mrs Stoddart of Primrose Hill in 1904 offered the school several articles of interest from South Africa. There must have been quite a lot of items as a new glass cabinet was required. It is unknown whether the lady had returned from a holiday there or had spent several years abroad.

A more needful gift was presented to the school in 1909 - a set of Chambers Encyclopaedias of 10 volumes with a suitable oak cabinet. The chairman of the school board (Mr G L Moffat) expressed the Board's high appreciation of the handsome and useful gift and stated that it was worthy of their appreciation: "All the more because it had been voluntarily presented."

The gift came from Dr J Coates of Paisley (the manufacturers' of cotton thread).

On the 20th November 1931 the Headmaster: "Received from Mr W Donaldson, Dar-Es-Salaam, section of the tree under which Stanley met Livingstone." No one knows what happened to this historical relic or why Lockerbie was singled out as the recipient.

Prizes were established by the School board as early as 1876. One of these was The Courtesy Prize in 1904, but prizes were also donated often in memory of a deceased person.

The Sheena Cormack Memorial Prize in November 1931 for a pupil in the infant department was established by Mr and Mrs David Cormack, Royal Bank House, in memory of their daughter who had died in June.

In 1898 a letter from the secretary of the London Dumfriesshire Association was received containing a prize for the best arithmetician in school. In 1899 it was awarded to James R Smith.

A prize was awarded by Charles Stewart of 38 Eaton Place, London (nephew of the late C Stewart of Hillside) for the best essay on "The Attractions of Rural Life". The prize in 1905 was won by William Wright of Howgillside.

William Sanders of Rosebank, who was the chairman of the school board, donated a medal for achievement. In 1928 the recipient was William Maxwell who studied medicine in Edinburgh and served in the RAMC during World War Two.

Another recipient of that medal was Ted Hills in 1963. The original dies for the William Sanders Medal were located in Edinburgh and are used for the Dux and Proxime Accessit in the present Celebration of Achievement.

Books were often given as prizes. The 1905 prize for attendance was a novel by the legendary Annie S Swan - no doubt full of old fashioned morality. The prize-winner was Grace Harkness. Another was won by her relative Bessie in 1915.

Prizewinners Lockerbie Academy and Lockerbie Primary 1963
Back Row L-R: Jim Fleming (Junior Boys Sports Champion), Liz Murdoch (Senior Girls Sports Champion),
Billy Brown (Senior Boys Sports Champion and Captain Kirtle House), Vera Hume (Captain Kirtle House Champions)
Second Row L-R: Janet Jamieson, Allan Pagan (Captains Criffel House Primary Sports Champions), Sandra Nairn (Proxime Accessit),
Ted Hills (Sanders Dux Medal), Liz Findlater (Junior Girls Sports Champion)
Front Row L-R: Vivienne Armstrong (Best Girl Infant Dept), Andrew McCall (Best Boy Infant Dept), Donald Fraser (Dux Primary School)

Due to rising costs books gave way to certificates. The recipient of this one shown here was Mary Graham.

The school assembly hall displays the dux boards showing the names of duxes since 1908. There were none for a period of time in the 1970s and 80s or even prizegivings as they were seen at the time, politically, to be elitist, however these have been reinstated by Graham Herbert.

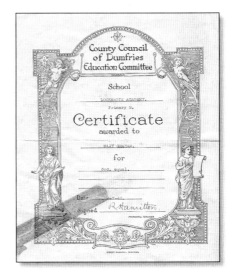

Mary Graham's School Certificate 1942

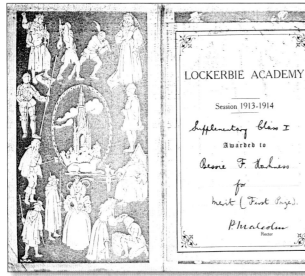

Bookplate used in Bessie Harkness' Prize

Behaviour having collected praise stamps for this throughout the session. In addition to these prizes are the cups and shields presented for sporting successes.

The school itself has won awards and competitions for example:-

The log book entry of 26th March 1911: "Daily Record £1000 competition for children has been

Sports Shield

At an annual Celebration of Achievement evening (costs more than £2k to stage and pay for prizes etc.) in June, pupils can be awarded certificates for subjects as well as for Endeavour or Good completed by thirty pupils and the standard of their work is distinctly good."

DUX MEDAL		DUX MEDALLI		DUX MEDAL	
1908	ROBERT McLEAN	1928	WILLIAM MAXWELL	1948	IAN F. GORDON
1909	MARGARET K. BROATCH	1929	WATSON C. BELL	1949	ISOBEL HUME
1910	ROBERT MACKIE	1930	JENNY K. MAXWELL	1950	IAN B. ROBERTSON
1911	HILDA BELL	1931	MARY ROSS	1951	MARY BEATTIE
1912	WILHELMINA R. BELL	1932	ALFRED L. SILLITTO	1952	HAZEL A. JEFFREY
1913	JOHN T. WILSON	1933	CATHERINE MACKIE	1953	MABETH BROWN
1914	RICHARD DINWOODIE	1934	HELEN D. HASTIE	1954	NEIL MACLEAN
1915	LEONORA JOHNSTONE	1935	JAMES J. ARMSTRONG	1955	PATRICIA A. ARRIS
1916	JOHN W.M. SCOTT	1936	EDWARD J. ARNOTT	1956	JOHN J. CARLYLE
1917	JOHN R. BROWN	1937	RICHARD M. SILLITTO	1957	E. ANNE DICKIE
1918	DOUGLAS BELL	1938	AGNES WOODBURN	1958	CHRISTOPHER R. HUGHES
1919	MARY H. BURNS	1939	JAMES MORRISON	1959	ALISON M. FELL
1920	MARGARET J. STOTHART	1940	ALEX MILNE	1960	SHEILAGH C. McNEIL
1921	ISABELLA R. WOOD	1941	ELLEN WOODBURN	1961	NO AWARD
1922	THOMAS R. BROWN	1942	JOYCE McQUILLIN	1962	M. HAZEL MILLER
1923	ANDREW R. HASTIE	1943	ELSPETH B. GASS	1963	EDWARD A. HILLS
1924	JAMES McCARLIE	1944	IRENE J. HAYNES	1964	NO AWARD
1925	JAMES PATTIE	1945	HECTOR J. HETHERINGTON	1965	NO AWARD
1926	ELIZABETH HENDERSON	1946	SHEENA McK. BEATTIE	1966	DAVID D. HALL
1927	PRIMROSE HENDERSON	1947	ANNE RAFFERTY		

Sections of School Dux Board

In 1931: " In a competition promoted by a French newspaper, published for schools, this school gained the second prize presented by the French Ministry of Education, and one of its pupils the fifth prize for individual pupils".

On the international front, Lockerbie has shown that it is no provincial backwater for educational achievements.

In 1998 pupil, Clare McEwan passed the International Baccalaureate Diploma with one of the highest scores in Europe- 43 out of 45 points- as well as gaining "A" passes in her Sixth Year Studies' examinations.

The following year Catriona Nichol was second runner up in an Essay contest organised by the Times and the Embassy of the Republic of Korea. The title was "Korea 2000: Youth Culture.

Michael Henderson, Head Boy, organised an appearance of Lockerbie Academy pupils in Jackie Bird's Let's Do the Show Right Here in 2002 and in 2006 , Lockerbie was a finalist in the Scottish Education Awards and appeared on the Fred McCaulay Show on Radio Scotland.

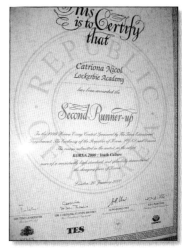

Korean Prize Essay

Lockerbie Academy has also been represented by prizewinning choirs

Lockerbie Academy EIS members were addressed by Miss Gerard in 1920 on 11th December on the "Educational Values of Music". She made a strong case for the study of music - not just singing - in the curriculum.

Lockerbie Academy Primary Choir c1960
L-R: 1, Jean Smith, Jean - ,Nancy Chambers, Jean Houston, 6,
John Jardine, Mary Spence, Allyson Reid, Linda Herrick,
Anne Bland and Douglas Fraser.

Junior Choir early 1960s
Mary Spence, Nancy Chambers, 3, Allyson Reid,
Linda Herrick, Jill Jackson, 7.

Senior Choice 1969
Back Row L-R: Janette Robb, Rosemary Sloan, Sheila Proctor, Heather Cameron, 5, Maureen Callender, Karen Currie, Carole Nutt
2nd Back Row: Ailsa Jackson, 2, Mary Carlyle, 3, 4, Ann Currie, Jean Houston, Ann Morton, Linda Herrick
3rd Row: Alison Morton, Lynna Baxter, Alison Reid, Joyce Burgess, Maureen Cambell, Elizabeth Mitchell, Audrey White, Iona Black, Una Irving
Front Row: Gwyneth Paterson, Glenda Moffat, Eileen Wilson, Rosemary Robinson, Jean -, Sheila Hyslop, 7, Elizabeth McCubbin. Teacher - Mr Reid.

Music festival - Scarborough fair 1991

33

CLASS PHOTOS
the 1900s to 1990s

1902

1911
Back Row: no 6 from left Jimmy Hunter;
Second Row: 1st left W Jardine, 5th is Andy Campbell and 7th is Ben Nutt;
Third Row: 1st Jim Jardine

1922
William Graham (3rd left in back row)

1926
Back Row L-R: Mic McGaw, Jim Thomson, Andrew Grieve, Lilly Napier, Mary Beattie, -Grierson, Jim Geddes, Boyd Johnstone, 9
Second Row L-R: 1, Willie Edgar, 3, 4, 5, Betty Hodge, 7, 8, 9,10
Third Row L-R: Mary Beattie, 2, Betty McLean, 4, 5, 6, Annie Jamieson, 8, 9, Jean Riddock
Front Row L-R: Jackie McClare, 2, Jack Varrie, Maxwell Rae, 5, 6, 7, 8, Jim White

1929
Back Row L-R: Hugh Cochrane, 2, 3, 4, Ian Callie, Willie Copeland, 7, Ian Brown
Second Row L-R: 1, Jim Haines, 3, Jim Stevenson, 5, Jim Geddes, Jackson Scott, Douglas Jardine
Third Row L-R: 1, Mary Beattie, Fizz, 4, 5, Betty Hodge, 7, - Green, 9, - McMilne
Fourth Row L-R: 1, Hettie Kerr, 3, 4, 5, 6, 7, Betty Ingles, Betty Lawrie
Front Row L-R: Bunty Campbell, Margaret Riddle, Gracie Reid, Margaret Scott, Nina Hunter, Jean Riddick

1929(2)
Back Row L-R: Tom Laurie, Matt Cochrane, Derek Simpson, Jack Kennedy, Robert Cochrane, Mic McGaw, Robert Adamson, Billy Fyfe
Second Row L-R: 1, 2, John Currie, 4, Frank Gibson, 6, 7, - Kirkpatrick, - Jamieson, - Johnstone
Third Row L-R: Annie Mills, 2, 3, 4, 5, 6, 7, 8, 9
Fourth Row L-R: 1, 2, - Jamieson, 4, 5, 6, Annie Scott, 8, 9
Front Row L-R: 1, - Sword, Mary Bell, 4, 5, 6, 7

1930

Back Row L-R: Jim Graham, Ian Lamb, 3, 4, 5, Michael Reid, Ian Latimer, Harmiston Irving, George Dempster
4th Row: 1, Gordon Paterson, John Carruthers, -Wilson, Doug Crowley, David Edwards,
John White, 8, - Kennedy, David Lockhart, Isobel Stodart
3rd Row: 1, Graham Bell, -Slaven, Anna McCallum, Walter Wightman, Billy Galloway, 7, Billy Brockbank,
Matty Cameron, Isobel Richardson, Renwick McArthur, -Strong
2nd Row: 1, 2, 3, Sarah Geddes, 5, Dorothy Kirkpatrick, 7, Crystal Robinson, Sarah McBride, 10
At front: Betty Williamson, - Campbell, Julia Carruthers.

1931

Back Row L-R: Ian McLean, Robert Jardine, Campbell Henry, David Stevenson, John Sneddon and Bobby Kirkwood
Third Row L-R: Jack Holt, Alec Gardiner, John Brown, Boyd Kelly, Jas Stevenson, John White
Second Row L-R: Mollie Smith, Katherine Reid, Cathy MacMillan, Jeanette Green, Margaret Howie
Front Row L-R: Helen Hastie, Betty Henderson and Betty McLean

c1933
Back Row L-R: George Carruthers, 2, Ian Stewart, 4, Bert Kelly, 6, 7, John Shennan, Tommy Richardson
3rd Row: John Jamieson, 2, - Gibson, John Muir, 5, 6, - McBride, Jim McGregor, Jack Jamieson
2nd Row: 1, - Paterson, 3, 4, 5, Nettie Richardson, 7, 8, 9, Mary Beattie
Front Row: Billy Dunbar, Billiy McKie, Moira MCardle, 4, Nora Coppola, 6, 7, Hamish Campbell, Peter McGregor

1934/5
Back Row L-R: 1, Jim Richardson, 3, George Brown, 5, 6, 7
Second Row L-R: 1, - Scott, Jim Turnbull, 4, Matt Cochrane, Tom Laurie, - Branny, 8, 9
Third Row L-R: 1, Gracie Reid, 3, Jenny Geddes, 5, 6, Ella Lockhart, 8, - Nicholson
Front Row: Not known

c1937
Back Row L-R: Billy Grieve, 2, 3, 4, 5
4th Row: Dennis Pringle, 2, Eric Scott, Cecil Begg, Keith Leitch, 6, -Kinleyside,-Kinleyside
3rd Row: 1, Ronnie Graham, Ian Dorian, Billy Anderson, Eric Gibson, Ian McQueen, 7, Ronnie Bell, Henry Jackson, John Johnstone
2nd Row: Mary Inglis, 2, 3, Sheena Irving, Nancy Wilson, Margaret Davidson, Sheila McKenzie, Nan Campbell, 9, 10, Cathie Thomson
Front Row: no names

1940s
Back Row L-R: Bertie Coppola, Adam Dickson, Jim Scott, 4, George Hunter, Eddie Swan, 7, John Davidson
4th Row: 1, 2, Margery Richardson, 4, Ann Currie, Barry Corser, 7, 8, 9
3rd Row: Isobel Halliday, Sheena Stewart, 3, George Mundell, Eric Gibson, 6, David Morrin, Ronald Dow, 9, Margaret Coates
2nd Row: 1, 2, 3, 4, 5, 6,Rose McArdle, Isla Little, -Morton, Jessie Brown, Pearl Burnside
Front Row: Ronnie Callender, Nancy Gardiner, Rena Gass, 4 , Sheila McKay, Ann Beattie, 7, 8

1940s

1940s

1943
Back Row L-R: H Rogerson, B McMillan, R Bell, John Nutt, -Burnie, -Waterston -Mills
2nd Row: G Binns, Sheena Beattie, Ola Richardson, Grace Smith, 5
3rd Row: Jessie Moffat, Shirley Murray, Barbara Buckle, Frances Relph, Pat Templeman,
Margaret Wylie, Eileen Paterson, Ray Shankland
4th Row: Jean Kelly, Alice Graham, Irene Haynes, Lorna Varrie, Jean McQuillan, Betty Jardine, Evelyn Lockhart, Elsa Templeton
Front Row: Isobell Wilson, Annie Beck

P4 1944 (53 pupils)
Back Row L-R: William Oliver, A Johnstone, David Knox, A McKay, E Irving, P Carruthers, J Lyons, J Stewart
Second Row L-R: -Stanton, Jack Gass, W McKerlie, A Graham, W Scott, I Wyllie, R Vernon, J Cameron, R Bisset, G Shearer, D Bell
Third Row L-R: D Bovill, E Roddick, H Dunbar, G Gardiner, H Mills, I Dickson, N Johnstone,
M Harvey, J Anderson, C Murphy, S McArthur, L Stevenson, J Rae,
Fourth Row L-R: E Newbigging, V Waugh, M Fingland, R Tait, G Richardson, M Nicholson,
C Shankland, B Miller, C Richardson, M Graham, 11
Front Row L-R: W Carruthers, J Campbell, D Bury, H Forbes, V Johnstone, -Jardine, M Wilson, N Burnside, A Varrie, I Gordon.

1944 Qualifying class
Back Row L-R: Ian Gordon, Jim Rae, George Shearer, Jim Richardson, Ian Wyllie, Billy Mearlie, Jack Gass, Jack Campbell
3rd Row: John Lyons, David Knox, Alan Johnstone,, Robert Vernon, Willie Oliver, James Stewart, Alan Graham, Robin Kerr
2nd Row: Lilian Stevenson, Hazel Forbes, Sheena McArthur, Jean Anderson, Helen Dunbar,
Pat Carruthers, Greta Gardiner, Mary Graham, Margaret Templeton, Irene Dickson, Dorothy Bury
Front Row: Vera Waugh,Ethel Newbiggin, Grace Richardson, Betty Carlyle, Roy Bisset, Moira Fingland, -Johnstone, Clara Shanklin,
Chrissie Murphy. Seated in front: 1 , Nan Burnside, Evelyn Roddick

c1944
Back Row L-R: 1, 2, 3, - Kinleyside, 5, Ronnie Graham
3rd Row: 1, 2, - Thomson, - Graham, Ian Dow, Willie Jardine, 7, Dorothy Anderson, 9
2nd Row: - Smith, 2, - Sloan, Billy Grieve, Billy Anderson, 6, Jim Scott, 8
Front Row: 1, 2, 3, 4, 5, 6, Jean Carlyle, Betty Wright, Nan Campbell

1945

Back Row L-R: Bobby Matthews, Jim Nutt, Alistair Richardson, 4, Dick Bell, Gordon Irving, George Mundell, B Lindsay
2nd Row: 1, Bill Elliot, George White, Arron Carruthers, 5, Jim Smith, Ian Davidson, Kenny Hunter, 9, Dick Wallace, Ann Rafferty
3rd Row: - Bell, 2, - Kerr, Marjory Richardson, - Dempster, George Beattie, Sally Bryden, - Swan, Jenny McLaren, Francis Rogerson, - Wright
4th Row: Alex Clark, 2, Irene Wallace, - Johnstone, 5, 6 ,7, Margaret Coates, Eva Mckenzie, 10, Jim Scott
Front Row: 1, Will Davidson, Marjory McMichael, 4, Nancy Inglis, -Irving, Jim Jardine, 8

P5 10 year olds about 1946

Back Row L-R: Jackie Swan, Robert McAdam, Alec Paterson, Kenneth McKenzie, 5, John Beattie, Martin Oliver, Tom Corrie, 9
4th Row: John Dickson, Douglas Roxburgh, Bob Gracie, Jim Kelly, Tony Murray,
Willie Linton, Charlie Johnstone, George McKinnon, Jack Gray, Maxwell Kerr
3rd Row: Mary Mason, Suzanne Mollison, Margaret Carruthers, Betty Adamson,
Kathleen Morton, Jean Notman, Mary Johnsone, 8, Phyllis Hunter, 10, Esther Anderson
2nd Row: Olive Cannon, Olive Broatch, Isobel Kerr, May Starkey, Shirley Murray,
Pamela Robertson, Primrose Grieve, Elizabeth Smith, Eileen Hood, Janet Templton, 11
Front Row: Bill Muir, Roy Bell, John Moffat, Doreen Jamieson, Ian Jackson, Bert Waugh, Willie Nicol.

c 1947
Back Row L-R: Jack Campbell, Jean Sloan, Billy, McEarlie, Margaret Anderson, Robert Vernon, 6, Jim Murray
3rd Row: Douglas Bell, Michael Carruthers, Alan Johnstone, William Armstrong,
John Gilmour, William Oliver, Adam Shannon, Roy Kirkpatrick
2nd Row: Margaret Pattie, Hazel Forbes, 3, 4, 5, Irene Dickson, 7, Dorothy Bury,- Grant
Front Row: Jim Copeland, Ian Armstrong, Alan Brown.

1948 Class 3AB
Back Row L-R: Alec Varrie, Jack Gass, Evelyn Roddick, Margaret Wightman, Ian Gordon, John Boyce
Middle Row L-R: John Johnstone, Colin Murray, Alan Graham, Pat Carruthers, David Knox, John Lyons, James (Bunny) Lamont
Front Row L-R: Lilian Stevenson, Mary Graham, Clara Shankland, Helen Dunbar, Grace Richardson,
Isobel Dalgleish, Ethel Newbigging, Greta Gardiner, Jean Armstrong.

1949 1st year class
Back Row L-R: Greta Stevens, Greta Coupland, Maisie Johnstone, Betty Adamson,
Pamela Robertson, Jean Creighton, Olive Broatch, Margaret Bell, Dorothy Holt, Eileen Hood.
3rd Row: John Dickson, Tom Johnstone, Martin Oliver, John Beattie, Jackie Swan, Charlie Johnstone,
Bert Daly, Donald Henderson, Eric Carson, Alex Hunter, Douglas Roxburgh
2nd Row: Mona McCallum, Elizabeth Smith, Margaret Carruthers, June Kerr, Mary Beattie, Anne Mason,
Margaret McWhitock, Doreen Jamieson, Margaret Gardiner, Janet Hodgson, Jean MacLellan.
Front Row: Ronnie Robertson, John McWhir, David Porteous, Kenneth Sherry, 5, -Russell.

1949/50
Back Row L-R: Murray Forbes, John Graham, Donald Myatt, David Whitelaw, Eric Nutt,
Neil Swanston, Robert Nicholson, Robert Shaw, Frank Farrell
2nd Row L-R: Andrew Jardine, Robert Gardiner, Jimmy Richardson, John Templeton, James Buchanan,
Robert Clydesdale, Douglas Rush, Peter Patterson, 9, Raymond McGarr, Bobby Craig
3rd Row: Edith Chambers, - Lockhart, 3, - Jeffrey, Ishbel McKay, - Barratt, - Craig, June Scott, Julia Irving, Etta Jardine, Amy Johnstone
Front Row: Sheena Maltman, Eileen Gordon, Jennifer Wilson, - Grierson, - Carmichael,
Gwyneth Gass, Elizabeth Hogg, Marjory Dyer, Chrissie Halliday, Elizabeth Brockbank

1949-52?
Back Row L-R: Willie Nichol, 2, Neil Swanston, 4, 5, 6, 7, 8, - Jackson
Second row L-R: 1, 2, Eileen Gordon, 4, 5, 6, 7, 8, 9, Hector McLean
Third Row L-R: Alec McLintock, Maureen Ronnie, 3, 4, 5, 6, 7, 8, 9,10, Ian Nicholson
Front Row L-R: 1, 2, 3, 4, James McGhie, Tom Ray, 7, Adam Carruthers, - Nichol

1951
Back Row L-R: Mona McCallum, Betty Adamson, Alec Hunter, Bert Daly, Charlie Johnstone, Anne Mason, Eileen Hood
2nd Row: Ronnie Robertson, Jackie Swan, Tom Johnstone, Mary Beattie, Pamela Roberston,
Margaret Carruthers, Douglas Roxburgh, Martin Oliver, John Dickson
2nd Row: Greta Stevens, Jean Creighton, Dorothy Holt, Margaret Gardiner, Doreen Jamieson,
Jean McLellan, June Kerr, Olive Broatch
Front Row: Kenneth Sherry, John McWhir, David Porteous.

1951 - 1953
Only name is Winston Nelson second row from back 1st left

1953
Back Row L-R: S Graham, W Masterson, M Gordon, S Creighton, 5, W McDermont, S Maxwell
Middle Row: A Smyllie, M Graham, K Morrison, J McWhir, W Barbour, J Mason, J Graham, K Robertson, W Lawson
Front Row: S Hood, H Telfer, N Grierson, M Hannah, R Burns, H Robertson, M Hamilton, J McMillan

Class 1B 1964
Back Row L-R: Irving Davidson, Brian Moffat, Brian Ferguson, Harry Earl,
Duncan Greig, Sandy McLean, Frank Wright, Gordon Pringle, David Scott
Middle Row: Tom Roehricht, Bobby Thorburn, Colin McCourt, Irene Wilson, Helen Thompson,
Janice Bell, Margaret Thomson, Anne Wells, Neil Donaldson, David Rogerson, Peter Carruthers
Front Row: Liz Tait, Pearl McGaw, Mary Carlyle, Marjory Crossan, Mary Copland, Anne Wyllie, Janet Howatson, Lynna Baxter

Class 1A 1965
Back Row L-R: Andrew Hillier, Ian McKilligan, David Creelman, Keith Hunter, Raymond Fletcher, Ian McDonald, Kenny Spence, Ian Steele
2nd Row: Angus Traill, Anthony Dinwoodie, Una Irving, Heather Cameron, Joan Ritchie, Rae Rankine, Andrew Miller, Wilson Campbell
Front Row: Julia Carruthers, Isabelle Wilson, Karen Currie, Carole Nutt, Isabel Pattie, Mary Gass, Kate Smith, Glenda Moffat, Jean Moffat

3AB Girls 1968
Back Row L-R: Angela Tweddle Joan Ritchie, Eileen Mackie, Vicky Brunt, Carole Nutt, Heather Cameron, Janetta Robb, Karen Currie
Mid Row: Una Irving, Kate Smith, Agnes Rogerson, Maureen Callendar, Pat Irving, Irene Rogerson, Rosemary Sloan, Rosemary Carruthers
Front: Isabel Pattie, Glenda Moffat, Julia Carruthers, Mary Gass, Isabelle Wilson, Margaret McNeish, Elizabeth Mitchell, Rena Finlay.
Absent Rae Rankine, Judith Barclay

4AB Girls 1969
Back Row L-R: Pat Irving, Judith Barclay, Maureen Callendar, Angela Tweddle, Eileen Mackie, Rena Finlay, Rosemary Sloan
Mid Row: Rosemary Carruthers, Rae Rankine, Una Irving, Irene Rogerson, 5, Karen Currie,
Carole Nutt, 8, Vicky Brunt, Joan Ritchie, Kate Smith, Agnes Rogerson
Front Row: Isabelle Wilson, Mary Gass, Miss Pont, Miss Mackay, Glenda Moffat, Isabel Pattie

1969 Girls 3A-C
Back Row L-R: Hazel McGarva, Margaret Hoffman, Anne Farish, Elma Davidson, Anne Armstrong,
Margaret Crossan, Margaret Kean, Kate Byers, Irene Cook, Jean Gray, Sheelah Sloan, Jennifer Smith
Middle Row: Elizabeth Carruthers, Norah Edgar, Maureen Lowe, Moyra Deans, Lesley McInnes, Iona Black, Mairi Campbell,
Rosemary Reid, Anne Riding, Lynda Campbell, Alison Munro, Gina Scott, Shona Robison, Elizabeth Hope, Isobel Jackson, Mary Finlay.
Front Row: Janice Ferguson, Sheila Coupland, Angela Brown, Violet Little, Caroline Starkey, Linda Shearer,
Mrs Lockhart, Mr Martin, Miss Mackay, Pamela Dempster, Margaret Gray, Donna Thompson, Grace Leopold, Fiona Sloan.

Class S1 c1970
Back Row L-R: David Telfer, John Jackson, Jim Carruthers, Andrew Campbell, Gary Smith, David Taylor, John Whittaker;
3rd Row: Leona Crawford, 2, Kirsty Mackie, Eileen Mundell, Ruth Lennox, Kay Black, - Wilson,
Hazel Armstrong, Sheila -, 10, Mary McGarr, Karen Stevens, 13
2nd Row: Dot Purslow, Eva Oswald, - White, 4, Catriona Robertson, 6, 7, Alison Irving, Kate Ramsden
Front Row: Eric Armstrong, 2, Derek Mundell, David Mahon, Drew Burgess, Stephen Wilson.

5th year Boys 1970
Back Row L-R: John Rogerson, John Hepburn, Gordon Maxwell, Andrew Hillier, Keith Borthwick,
Morris McSkimming, Ian McKilligan, Malcolm Scott, Andrew Miller, Ian Beck
Mid Row: Frankie Jackson, Ian Steele, James Twidale, David Graham, Robert Hendrie, Robert Gibson,
Tony Finlay, Ian Telfer, Andrew Roberston, Michael Stuart
Front Row: Alastair Wilson, Keith Hunter, 3, 4, Anthony Dinwoodie, Billy Howatson, Ian Glendinning, David Creelman, Kenneth Hart

Kirtle Class c 1970s
Back Row L-R: Iain Cruikshank, Andrew Dunbar, Thomas Grant, Jim Manson, Gordon Rae, Michael Irving, David Robson, Gary Crowley
3rd Row: Janette Kerr, Audrey Gardiner, Lorraine Glendinning, Christine Lockhart, Shona Hill, Fiona Little, Cindy Davies, Sandra Crawford
2nd Row: Isobel Rodger, Karen Lamont, Karen Hogg, Fiona Watson, Heather Richardson, Marian Coupland,
Sandra Gass, Linda Varrie, Audrey Bell, Karina Warbeck, Eilidh Hannah
Front Row: Neil Ferbie, Graeme McKilligan, Colin Nichol, David Birch, Douglas Stephen, Maxwell McCall, Sam Dalgleish,
George Clow, John Irving. Absent Reg Turner. Teacher Arthur Johnstone.

Class 1C Kirtle 1970-71
Back Row L-R: James Davies, Colin Riddet, Colin Kerr, Ian Sword, Gerald McDonald,
Joseph Gilmour, Fraser Geekie, Nigel Anderson, Michael Currie
Mid Row: John Lockerbie, Patrick Morris, Neil Gibson, Lindsay Wright, Elizabeth Marshall,
Wilma Carlyle, Frank Smith, Alan Sloan, David Gibson
Front Row: Janette Branny, Jaqueline Nicol, Jay Little, Sheila Scott, Maureen Steele,
Shona Bridges, Shona Creelman, Christine Hinselwood, Jane Scott.
Teacher Mr Johnstone. Missing Amy Mason and Gary Saunders.

Class VI 1971
Back Row L-R: Tony Finlay, Ian Steel, Ian McKilligan, David Graham, Ian Telfer, Ian Beck, Robert Hendrie,
Andrew Miller, Michael Stuart, James Twidale, Malcolm Scott, Anthony Dinwoodie, Frank Jackson
Mid Row: Linda Young, Una Irving, Lorna Bell, Kathleen Chalmers, Ann Elliot, Helen Murray, Eileen Mackie, Christine Taylor,
Joan Ritchie, Violet Laidlaw, Elizabeth Little, Sylvia Little, Kate Smith, Ann Nichol, Sheila Bell, Rae Rankine, Isabelle Wilson
Front Row: Isabel Pattie, Robert Gibson, Maureen Callendar, Billy Howatson, Carole Nutt, John Rogerson, Agnes Rogerson,
Kenneth Hart, Karen Currie, David Creelman, Rosemary Sloan, Ian Glendinning.
Absent: Gordon Maxwell, Andrew Robertson, Morris McSkimming, Keith Borthwick, John Hepburn,
Alastair Wilson, Andrew Hillier, Murray Irving, Ian Reeve, David Paterson, Rosemary Watson, Susan Duddy

c1971/2
Back Row L-R: Tom Dow, Chris Armstrong, Walter Kennedy, 4, David Irving,
Norman McKay, Brian Templeton, Robin Thomson, Finlay McKenzie
Mid Row: Caroline Bone, Julie Iveson, Jackie Graham, 4, Susan Robertson, The twins, Yvonne-, Morag McKenzie
Front Row: 1, Julie Brownrigg, Lesley Allan, Lesley Thorburn, Alison Kaceden, Linda Wolff, 7, 8, 9 , 10,
Kneeling: Allan Burgess, 2, Paul Malner, Scott Mason, Ian Gibson

S5 1971/72 Girls
Amongst others are: Ann Spence, Sheila Hyslop, Margaret McDonald, Nancy Cameron, Carol Carruthers,
Eleanor Boa, Pat Kaceden, Joyce Burgess, Rosemary Robinson, Alison Morton, Lena Thomas,

3rd/4th Year 1972
Back Row L-R: David Omand, Alistair Martin, John Whittaker, Andrew Campbell, John Carruthers, David Taylor, Kenneth Hill
Middle Row: Stephen Wilson, Eva Oswald, Karen Stevens, Mhairi Telford, Sheila Lamont, Linda Jackson, Kay Black, Eileen Mundle, Alison Irving, Caroline Horn, Derek Mundle, Drew Burgess
Front Row: 1, Catriona Robertson, 3, 4, Kate Ramsden, Sybelle Kirkpatrick, - White, Hazel Armstrong, Doreen Graham

4th year boys 1974-5
Back Row L-R: Kenny Mitchell, Ian Hyslop, 3, 4, 5,Walter Kennedy, David Nutt,
Middle Row: Alastair Smith, Willie Drennan, 3, 4, Robert Jackson, Allan Burgess
Front Row: 1, Alan Barrie, Andrew Manson, Irving Mackay, Donald Donaldson, 6, Norman Mackay, Chris Armstrong

2nd/ 3rd year class of 1988
Back Row L-R: Tommy Callander, Paul -, Caroline -, Daniel -, Robin -,
Front Row: Heather McLatchie, Gary O'Neil, Jill Borthwick, David Wilson, Tammy Smith, Ian -, Heather -.

Class of 1993 Seniors
Back Row L-R: Ross Wyllie, Laura Burgess, Ben Hann, Gordon Hill, Stephen Dorrance, Duncan Spence,
Stuart Griffin, Steven Callender, Derek Robson, Lesley Moffat, Jill Hutchison
2nd Back Row: Diane Brown, David Brown, Allan Graham, John Muir, Ross Morrin, Daniel Long,
Stuart Carruthers, Tim Jones, Fraser Wyllie, Douglas Thomson, Tom Kemp, Robbie Hislop
3rd Back Row: Tina Lockhart, Nichola Houston, Claire Little, Mary Little, Soraya Livingston, Ruth Scott,
Audrey McMinn, Jan Cairney, Diane Sutherland, Katy Smith, Carolyn Hills
Second Front Row: Claire Bryce, Tamlyn Smithers, Joanne McGarrie, Karen Turnbull,
Carole McArthur, Lyn Macrae, Kelly Walker, Caroline Fraser, Julie McMinn, Lesley Hunter, Kerry Basnett
Front Row: Scott Campbell, Cathy Irving, Matthew Orr, Arthur Johnstone, Sharon Little,
Headmaster Drew Blake, Gareth McIntyre, Gordon Ferrie, Rachel Harrison, Phil Quinn, Joanne Cooper

Bruges School Trip 1969

Ronald Watson, Robert Dirom, Jim Johnstone

Author is at the front

*Katherine Grant and
Fiona Griffin (1990/91)*

Trips and Treats

Christmas Treats

In 1907 The Dumfries and Galloway Advertiser recorded that Lady Buchanan Jardine: "Oversaw the entertainments for children from several schools who attended the parties at the town Hall in Lockerbie".

They started the afternoon with 2 plays, **"Creatures of Impulse"** and **"The Unhappy Princess"**. They then sang **"Hark the Herald Angels Sing"**; watched a demonstration dance of the Highland Fling and then proceeded to the recreation hall: "For an excellent repast". There were over 600 people, but the pupils who could not attend were to be forwarded their presents by their teachers. The presents were followed by the singing of the National Anthem.

In those days there was much "tugging of the forelock", but also reasons to be grateful for the bountiful food and presents when it was common for children to receive simply an orange and a sixpence in their Christmas stockings.

Christmas treats continued into the later part of the century with parties and dances organised in school and patrolled by teachers who were on the look out for alcoholic beverages hidden in coats and bags and other evidence of under age drinking.

John Little remembers that the 1970s disco music was brilliant, but the build up to the event was "naff" because for 4 to 5 weeks prior to the event there were dancing lessons in the gym during PE time. The dances, however, were not John Travolta style - they were Dashing White Sergeants and Eightsome Reels.

School trips

For many pupils school trips were the first chance to go abroad as foreign holidays for families were not so popular in the 1960s and 1970s partly because they were still very expensive.

The SS Uganda was regularly put into commission for school cruises.

The Baltic cruise in 1975 visited Denmark, Finland and Leningrad (now St Petersburg). The 60 pupils were looked after by only 4 teachers!

Uganda set sail from Dundee in June 1979 carrying Lockerbie pupils and calling at Rotterdam, Oporto, Gibraltar, Casablanca, Vigo before docking at Glasgow.

I remember the first time I had been abroad - the school trip to Belgium accompanied by Mr Hill and Mr and Mrs Wilson. We stayed in the beautiful town of Bruges and I remember visiting the WW2 cemeteries at Dunkirk. In my journal "My Trip" I see that I had written about visiting the Nunnery and several museums and a river boat trip, but I had not recorded the two things which were really memorable. The first was the awfully bad Channel crossing with loads of folk being sick and Mr Hill checking up on people asking how they were whilst munching a greasy hamburger roll. Rumours also abounded

that the ferry had sank on its return to England! We were quite oblivious to the panic at home when parents heard the extremely bad weather reports from the English Channel. Mobile phones had not yet been invented.

The other great memory of that trip was coming home just in time to watch the TV broadcast of the Moon Landing on July 1969.

School trip to Belgium 1969
Bruges - Carol, Gillian, Carole Nutt and Maureen Campbell

Nowadays the school regularly takes pupils to Belgium to visit the battlefields around Ypres and Paschendaele and the Commonwealth Grave Commission's cemeteries of World War One. Many come back from that trip moved by the experience. Several students take the opportunity to search for the graves of relatives or their names on the Menin Gate making the connection with that era even more poignant and relevant. Boys often linger over the graves of 15 year olds perhaps thinking that they could easily have been part of that "lost"generation of young men.

Now every second year the S1 and S2 pupils have the opportunity to improve their skiing as part of a residential course in Italy. There are often exchanges made with pupils from abroad. Countries such as Poland, Finland, Norway, Sweden and Italy have all been visited and students from these countries come to Lockerbie. In 1995 the school became the co-ordinating school in Comeniius an European Union project. The linked European awareness project has resulted in the production of a student newspaper, web site and conferences in Europe.

Cameron Murray reminisced about being part of the very first exchange with the Lycee Figeac organised by Bill Thompson. Another link is with the Gymnasium Padagogium in Bad Sachsa, Germany.

Under the direction of the present Senior Deputy Rector, Gordon Ferrie, the driving force behind

Gordon Ferrie

these European connections, the links are further enhanced by the use of technology. It is now possible for parents to see photographs 24 hours later by clicking on the school website www.lockerbie-academy.co.uk and following the link to Figeac Exchange. A "daily postcard" from trips can also be accessed so pupils can more closely keep in touch with their folks.

Visit by pupils from Bratislava, Finland, Norway, Poland to Lockerbie Academy 1995

1990 saw the first two Lockerbie students, Kathyrn Grant and Fiona Griffin, attend Syracuse University in New York State.

A list of all the Syracuse scholarship students is in the appendix.

Generally in the first half of the 20th century secondary pupils did not go on "field visits". This would be because times were financially bad in the 1920s and 1930s and also because of the war. Ian Nicholson did remember travelling to Glasgow to play in a football final where they "walloped" a Glasgow team, but he said they didn't go on any other visits.

In more recent times visits have been made to places of interest in England and Scotland. A memorable visit to Hadrian's' Wall was recorded by the local newspaper in 1969. The excuse was to learn more about the Romans to inform our understanding of Latin'. The weather was suitably a continental

heat wave with the resultant sunburnt necks causing sickness in the bus on the way home.

Visits were and are still made to Universities' open days as are the theatre trips to the Lyceum in Edinburgh. This was a grand opportunity to see young (and soon to be famous) actors on stage. The Crucible. Macbeth and the Changeling were all eagerly attended in the 1960s.

We didn't actually see Sir Laurence Olivier in the flesh, but he was "blacked up" as Othello in the film we viewed at the Theatre Royal in Dumfries also in the 60s.

Concert trips were organised by enterprising pupils in 1969-70. Ian Steele remembers the great deal of preparation that went into the very successful excursions to Edinburgh, Glasgow and Newcastle. Who else can remember seeing Marc Bolan sitting elf - like cross-legged on the stage of the Usher Hall; Jethro Tull; The Nice with Keith Emerson playing the Usher Hall Organ; Ten Years After and The Incredible String Band? Those were the days when we dressed in maxi skirts, loon pants and velvet jackets, wearing beads and flowers in our hair. They were great fun and a super chance for us living in a rural area to see some of the best bands of the era. A then unknown Tony Blair is recorded as having attended some of these same concerts as no doubt an escape from his boarding school routine at Fettes College.

LOCKERBIE ACADEMY PUPILS VISIT HADRIAN'S WALL

JUNE 69

A party of 37 senior pupils from Lockerbie Academy, under the over-all supervision of Mr John Gair, Head of the History Department, and accompanied by Mr Brown and Miss Mackay, visited Hadrian's Wall on Thursday.

The first stop was at Housesteads Fort, the most interesting example of a wall fort. After examining the remains of the granaries, barracks, gateways and the commander's house, the party walked along the famous remaining section of the wall to Cuddy's Crag, studying a milecastle on the way. Afterwards, they visited the small museum where they saw carved stones, fragments of pottery, tiles and other articles, which had been found during excavations, as well as models of the fort as it was in Roman times.

Following a picnic lunch, the party moved on to the Temple of Mithras at Carrawburgh Fort, and from there to the Bridge Abut - ment opposite Chesters Fort. This

was followed by a brisk walk to Brunton Turret, and thus the party was able to study examples of all three types of military buildings constructed behind the wall.

The visit was enhanced by brilliant Mediterranean sunshine, which produced some Roman-type suntans.

Newscutting - visit to Hadrian's Wall 1969

Royal Lyceum

The Royal Lyceum Theatre Edinburgh

THE CHANGELING

by
THOMAS MIDDLETON and **WILLIAM ROWLEY**

Directed by	RICHARD EYRE
Designed by	JOHN GUNTER
Lighting by	ANDY PHILLIPS
Choreography by	LINDSAY KEMP
Music by	ADRIAN SECCHI

CAST:

The Castle

Beatrice-Joanna	ANNA CALDER-MARSHALL
Vermandero, father to Beatrice	BROWN DERBY
De Flores, servant to Vermandero	DAVID BURKE
Alonzo de Piracquo, suitor to Beatrice	DENIS LAWSON
Tomazo de Piracquo, brother to Alonzo	FRANK MOOREY
Alsemero, a nobleman, afterwards married to Beatrice	ARTHUR COX
Jasperino, his friend	TOM WATSON
Diaphanta, maid to Beatrice	CLEO SYLVESTRE

The Madhouse

Alibius, a jealous doctor	MARTIN HELLER
Isabella, his wife	KATE BINCHY
Lollio, his servant	JOSEPH GREIG
Antonio, a changeling	ROLAND CURRAM
Pedro, friend to Antonio	MICHAEL HARRIGAN
Franciscus, a counterfeit madman	JOHN SHEDDEN
Servants and Madmen	IAIN AGNEW SANDRA BUCHAN CLARIS ERICKSON IAN IRELAND JEREMY CHANDLER BILL McCABE

The action takes place in the Spanish seaport of Alicante.

There will be one interval of fifteen minutes

Credits :
We would like to acknowledge the assistance of :—
West Bow Gallery ;   Unicorn Antiques, Dundas Street ;
Museum of Childhood, High Street ; Wardrobe Care by Daz.

Programme for "The Changeling" 1970 with some now famous names

The newspaper cutting featured below describes how Dumfries Local Conservative Club played host on Saturday mornings to young people who wished to "Disco". Some Lockerbie Academy pupils are seen here enjoying themselves, having travelled from Moffat that morning! This must have been some sort of political initiative to entice young people off the streets of Dumfries.

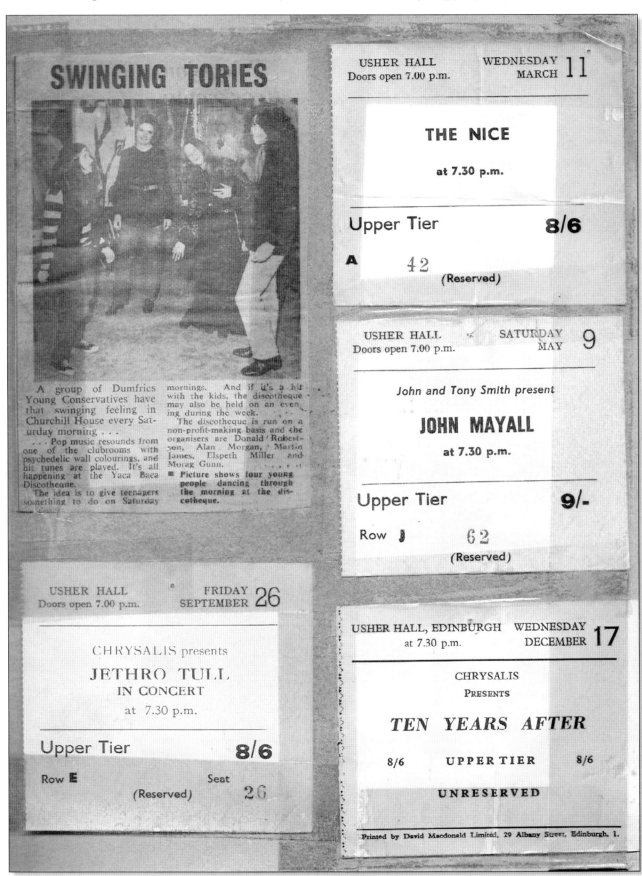

A page from a former LA pupil's scrapbook revealing the range of concerts organised by pupils themselves in 1969/70

Attendance

Lockerbie Academy does its best to combat truancy and maintain full attendance. However, it would seem that it was more of a problem in the 19th century. Her/His Majesty's Inspectors; members of the school board and later deputations from the council came regularly to the school to check the figures for attendance.

Concerns over poor attendance figure greatly in both the Headmasters' log books and the Minutes of the School Board.

Parents were called in front of the Board to explain why they were keeping their children away from school. They had to have good reasons. Sometimes it was simply because they could not afford to pay the school fees. These poorer parents were then directed to the Parochial Board to request help.

My grandmother often used to say to me, when my parents had spent a sum of money on me, that: "I'd see them in the puir hoose"!*. Such was the fear and shame of that institution even though it had disappeared before I was born!

Other parents kept their offspring away from school because they needed them to look after siblings (families were generally very much larger in Victorian times - 10-14 children was not uncommon) or to go out to work to augment the meagre family income. There was no social security and it was often hard for families to make ends meet and with wages being low, every little helped. The Board would impose fines on these defaulting parents.

In 1920 the school dux, Margaret Jane Stodhart had a remarkable attendance record. Margaret from Ecclefechan, during 12 years of school, had only been absent once and that was due to a railway strike when it was too wet to cycle!

Farm work

Living in a rural area most pupils stayed on or near farms and farm work was often a cause of absence. Up until the 1940s most farms were not mechanised and farmers required lots of hands especially at busy times such as the harvest or the Tattie Picking.

These extracts from the first school log book illustrate this well.

1874 April to June : "Several pupils leaving for the summer work".

Sept 12th: "Attendance on the whole good. There are still, however, somewhere about 120 absentees on account of harvest operations".

May 25th 1876: "Tomorrow being the term day the school will not be opened. Many of the senior pupils now leaving school in order to be engaged in agricultural work".

The school board reported in June that : "Attendance thinner and thinner, report of irregular attendance of several pupils handed to the officer of the School Board to be submitted to the Attendance Committee".

Oct 20th: "Attendance this week not quite so good, potato lifting being considered the season".

Oct 26 "Annual holiday. Hiring market."

April 12th 1878: "Attendance thin, very much interfered with by the Agricultural Show, and the Lockerbie Steeple Races".

Oct 18th 1878: "On account of a number of sheep sales and markets being held this week, attendance has been very irregular".

April 18th 1879: "Attendance during the week somewhat irregular on account of the annual April Cattle Show".

Sept 26th: "Attendance very much interfered with during the week on account of a great lamb sale being held and the September Hill Market taking place on Thursday".

Exasperation is noted by Mr Palmer, below, as he would have had to explain the attendance figures to the School Board rather like present Heads having to meet targets. The "whipper-in" or attendance officer was finally called:-

26th Oct 1883: "On Monday last, 32 Standard boys were absent from school - reported by officer to be "beating" for coursing meeting this week."

In 1898 the Clerk of the School Board was instructed to let parents know that he would: "Write to the employers of these pupils who were engaged at harvest work, pointing out that they rendered themselves liable to prosecution under the Education Act".

In the 20th century during both world wars there was a need for people to grow their own food and "Dig for Victory"; farmland was intensively cultivated; some workers were enlisted into the armed forces and it became necessary for the farmers to get help, but by this time it was more regulated and Eileen Scott, the Secretary in the 1940s, remembers farmers queuing outside the school for willing hands whilst she had to give out time sheets and allocate the pupils to the farmers, sometimes groups of 30 for each of the big farms.

Sanctioned Absences

Perhaps the headmasters realised that there would inevitably be absences for rural events such as the Hiring Fairs and it would be more practical to approve a holiday in advance.

1st Sept 1887: "This being the Annual Agricultural and Horticultural Show, and being held on the school premises, the classes did not meet."

27th April 1911: " Half day holiday granted for Lockerbie hiring fairs".

April 1926: "Half day holiday for Hiring Fair".

On these days landowners, tenant farmers and farm hands would meet in the town to sign leases and exchange terms of employment and seek new work or workers. This could mean families moving from say the Lochmaben area to Ecclefechan

*Puir Hoose or poor house known as the workhouse in England.

which is quite a distance and would be daunting because the removals would be by horse and cart. These flittings would have had an impact on the school as pupils would be travelling from quite different parts of the parish or moving away altogether.

Other Holidays

Long ago there were lots of closures for events which would seem to us today to be unusual reasons for holidays.

In 1889 there was a holiday for pupils who were involved in singing in a ceremony for the opening of the Town Hall Buildings. The Board gave them a "Liberal treat " afterwards. (There is no indication of what the treat was.)

15th May 1891 "Half holiday granted this afternoon at request of a deputation of parents, who desired that the children might have an opportunity of visiting an entertainment for children in town for only one day".

The school was used for a polling station in the general election of 1900.

March 9th 1911: "School closed by request of the School Board to mark their appreciation of Sir Robert Buchanan Jardine's gift of a public park to Lockerbie. " A lovely gesture, but hardly a reason for a holiday!

Celebration of Royal occasions meant holidays for the children because royalty was much more revered one hundred years ago and Queen Victoria was very respected by many Scots. Her Jubilees were celebrated and her birthday became a holiday. Coronations, royal weddings and deaths were also commemorated with the Board allowing a holiday. Patriotism was expected and usually found.

Jan 23rd 1874: " Holiday today in honour of the Duke of Edinburgh's marriage". (This was Victoria's second son, Prince Alfred, who married a Russian Grand Duchess.)

Oct 30th 1874: "Holiday given yesterday and today, the former being the half year fair day, and the latter the occasion of laying the foundation stone of the new school buildings".

25th May 1882: "Gave a holiday for tomorrow for the Queen's birthday".

22nd June 1887: "Holiday yesterday in honour of the Queen's Jubilee". Victoria would have been on the throne 50 years.

In 1897 a petition was presented from certain pupils requesting an extended summer vacation in view of Her Majesty's Diamond Jubilee . In those days when women did not have the right to vote, it is remarkable that the petition was acknowledged, and accepted. The pupils must have thought that they were onto a winner, yet the Board was probably more conscious of the promotion of patriotism.

Three years later they approved another holiday: "For special circumstances this year, the Queen's birthday and the relief of Mafeking in the South African War." This was during the second Boer War and Mafeking was a welcome victory.

In 1901 the death of the Queen at Osbourne was noted in the Board Minutes on Tuesday Jan 22nd and the school pupils were given the afternoon off.

The coronation of King George V was made a holiday in 1911. (See photo below)

More patriotic enthusiasm was evident in May 1915 when the pupils were taken to a service in Dryfe Parish Church to hear lessons on " the Empire and Duties of Citizens". They were then given the afternoon off ; boys being offered a cricket match and the girls, a picnic in Lochmaben. Presumably this was to give them time to ponder on the world's events and perhaps pass on what they had learned to older brothers who might be encouraged to enlist in the army.

Headmaster Muir displayed his worries that attendance would be down again on July 6th 1876: "Sacramental holidays commencing this week, the attendance will be very much interfered with between now and the holidays" (Fast days

Lockerbie Academy celebrates the Coronation of King George V in 1911

were holidays too) and on Dec 26th 1878: "Attendance this morning so very poor that the usual Christmas holidays were given to extend to Jan 6th 1879". It will surprise readers that Christmas Day and Boxing Day were not recognised as holidays and yet religious days were closely observed in Victorian times.

Modern teachers will no doubt agree with their Victorian counterparts' views about the effects of the summer holidays:-

Sept 13th 1878: "The teachers report that during the long holiday, the pupils have forgotten their previous instruction to a great extent".

Weather

The weather also affected attendance. Floods, storms, ice and snow all caused havoc on the already poor country roads. Many children would not be able to get to school and those who generally walked would not dare set out on a five mile hike which might result in them being sent straight home.

These quotes indicate the severity of the weather.

16 Dec 1886: "Gave a skating holiday on Thursday afternoon".

Jan 28th 1901: "Snow lying and attendance poor in consequence".

Feb. 3rd 1911: "Half day holiday for skating".

Feb 18th 1929: "Two attendances marked consecutively to enable pupils to see something of the Waterloo Curling at Lochmaben - an event which has not taken place since 1908 on the Castle Loch".

Transport

As well as bad weather affecting roads and transport, the General Strike of 1926 made its impact on the school.

May 4th 1926: "Owing to stoppage of trains owing to the General Strike a large number of pupils are absent. Others managed to obtain motor conveyance, and a few cycle about 12 miles".

May 6th: "A bus service for bursars from Kirkpatrick Fleming has been arranged to start tomorrow, Friday at 8.30 am. It will pick up pupils from Gretna, Kirtlebridge, Eaglesfield, Waterbeck and Ecclefechan. Return service from school at 4.10pm".

Illness

Childhood illnesses were real causes for concern before the creation in 1947 of the National Health Service. Children died from illnesses which are not viewed today as particularly severe. Lack of medicine, damp housing, overcrowding and poverty all contributed to the appalling rates of infant mortality in Scotland.

April 9th 1875: "Heard that measles are in the district".

Throughout May measles was affecting attendance and by 28th May: "One third of the pupils now absent and the work of the school much interfered with".

This pattern continued until June 11th - a two-month epidemic with another three years later.

May 24th 1878: "Diphtheria reported this week, nearly 90 absentees".

On the 31st: "Cases of diphtheria increasing. Attendance very much affected. Today no fewer than 274 being absent".

On June 3rd: "Agreed to close the school for 3 weeks in consequence of the prevalence of diphtheria in the district".

The school reopened on August 6th 1878: "One or two cases of diphtheria still talked about" and even by 23rd Aug: "Several cases of diphtheria reported yet".

Nowadays diphtheria in this country is almost unheard of due to regular vaccinations, but it was highly contagious and could be fatal since there were no antibiotics available.

Other illnesses were common, greatly feared and life threatening:

Feb 4th 1876: "Two or three cases of scarletina reported in the town this week".

Jan 16th 1880: "Whooping cough and by the 30th: "Scarlet Fever."

Feb 13th: "During past week an average of 140 have been daily absent on account of measles". This went on until April 2nd: "Epidemics rapidly diminishing".

Then on June 4th mumps appeared and was still spreading by June 18th.

Sept 17th saw: "Scarlet fever reported'.

Scarlet fever or Scarlatina was associated with sore throats and a fever, a "strawberry" tongue and a fine rash over the upper body. It could be serious and often people's bedding and clothes were burned for fear of infection. Usually long periods of convalescence were needed so pupils could be absent for weeks.

The first Medical inspection took place on the 13th December 1897 so illnesses and medical problems could be identified, but sometimes that was all that happened as few parents could follow this up with medical attention as it was too costly.

Oct 1898: "An epidemic of measles - 350 from 659 attended".

The HMI report of 1912 mentions that children were still recovering from the effects of epidemic sickness..." The natural inertia and slowness of response of many children might be attributed to this cause... due regard has been paid to these circumstances". (Despite this the report was a damming one).

In 1914 Scarlatina in the neighbourhood affected staff too and in 1916 scarlet fever was reported and the school had to be disinfected. The infant department had to be closed for fourteen days.

Then the world-wide 'flu epidemic hit the country in 1918.

Before 1947 it was too expensive to call a doctor and so many people resorted to "Quacks" or pedlars of "universal" medicines designed or at least touted as "cure alls". Penicillin was not widely available until after the Second World War.

Polio was another feared infectious disease partly because no one seemed to know what caused it. Children were banned from public swimming pools as this was thought to be where the illness spread. In the early 1960s it was still common to see such children in callipers and some older people will remember the iron lung treatment. Vaccines were not fully developed until the 1950s.

Tuberculosis (otherwise known as consumption or Phthisis) was another common illness and school children spent long weeks recovering at Lochmaben Sanatorium. Patients had to be kept apart form others because TB could be spread by sneezes and water droplets. It affected the lungs and in the 1930s doctors prescribed fresh air. Beds being placed outside the wards on verandas. Pupils are now immunised with the BCG vaccine at school to prevent this debilitating and sometimes deadly disease.

One wonders how much schooling some children actually had.

In modern times notes for absences are required; regular patterns of inattendance and unsatisfactory explanations are investigated and letters sent home, but the causes are quite different. No longer are there Hiring Fairs; fewer pupils live on farms; fewer hands are needed for farm work; laws prevent underage working and laws set down the number of schooldays and holidays allowed. Roads are better and transport more reliable so it takes quite an unusual bout of bad weather to close the school.

Illness still causes absences, but the school has never again had huge epidemics requiring closure.

In the HMI report of 1993 the average school attendance was recorded as over 90% each week! Previous headmasters would not have believed it possible.

Indiscipline and Punishment

Many people have the view that In Victorian times Scottish school teachers were strict disciplinarians ready at all times to use the tawse and beat obedience into pupils. The result being that teachers were feared and schools were run like regiments with silence in every classroom and very few pupils daring to speak back to teachers.

Perhaps this was the case in some schools, and having read through Lockerbie's log books very few case of misdemeanour are recorded, yet the tone of each headmaster's notes do not seem unduly harsh.

When Mr Palmer became Headmaster in 1881 he distributed a new set of regulations to his staff.

"1 Corporal punishment to be inflicted as seldom as possible and chiefly for acts of insubordination, disobedience and continued wilful malattention.

11 Punishment for such offences, as lateness and non-preparation of home lessons to consist of detention after hours, under proper supervision - in the former case two minutes for every one late, and in the latter, the neglected work to be satisfactorily performed during the period of detention, Continued repetition of these offences to be reported to the headmaster, who will deal with these accordingly to his judgement.

111 Corporal punishment by any but the Headmaster to be limited to one stripe over each hand with the leather strap or 'tawse'- on no occasion is a pupil to be punished except over the hand, and any pupil who refuses to submit to punishment to be at once reported to the headmaster.

1V No pupil teacher or monitor to push, pull, or strike any of the pupils under any pretence whatever. The other teachers in each department will be expected to report at once every instance of infringement of this rule, which will be recorded in the log book."

The "belt" was acceptable as a form of punishment, yet this headmaster is very precise about when it could be used. Everybody knew exactly what they could and could not do.

He continued in the same manner - January 18th 1884:

"Gave elder pupils an address on 'manners'. Gave instructions to teachers to check all symptoms of rowdyism in the playground."

Three months later he noted in the log that he had dismissed two boys for insubordination and a year later another boy is dismissed for : "Insolent conduct towards Miss Roy". This boy had already used blasphemous language to Mr Craig two months earlier.

"Attendance much interfered with during the week by Circus in town. Punished a number of children absenting themselves without leave." Type of punishment is not mentioned.

There is little other mention of dismissals.

Headmaster Mr Malcolm in 1901 had to deal with : " A pupil in 4th year having left school on Friday afternoon without permission from headmaster or any responsible teacher was severely reprimanded today; she could give no explanation of her conduct."

In the 1912 HMI Report the comment is about some teachers: "Having a lot to learn in the art of class management. The practice of whispering answers should be firmly reproved"!

I found no mention of the class dunce or the dunce's cap nor was there mention of the punishment of standing in the corner. These probably did occur but would not have been seen as serious enough to be mentioned in the headmasters' logs.

In the first part of the 20th century former pupils talked about the belt and how often it was meted out to them and, in earlier decades, to their parents.

There was talk of teachers soaking their belts overnight in vinegar to harden them and make them more "effective". Some teachers - and not just the male ones - were particularly feared for their over exuberance with the belt. Many kept their belts hidden over their shoulders and under their academic gowns to more easily whip it out and thrash the desk to frighten a class into deathly silence and awe.

Pupils were often too scared to concentrate and learn for fear of making a mistake and being told to come out and be given "six of the best".

The tawse was banned in 1987.

Rulers rapped over knuckles, pieces of chalk thrown at sleepy heads, black board dusters flying across the classroom aimed at whisperers although legal at one time are now definitely not!

So what happens now? At least pupils are not punished for their ignorance of a subject. There is much more understanding of learning difficulties and no longer are left handed pupils forced to write with their right hands.

The quick sharp shock treatment has disappeared. In its place there are sanctions to encourage more appropriate behaviour as well as written exercises and detention and loss of privileges. Parents are involved quickly if things go wrong.

Pupils are not scared of teachers nowadays and most respond well to rules which are sensible. Discussion of rules is part of the Social Education programme. These rules when explained and understood encourage pupils to respect others and take responsibility. Treating people as you would expect to be treated yourself works and the vast majority of pupils behave well.

1952 Milk Sports' Champions
Sylvia Wyllie and Ian Graham.

Sports and games

Up until the 20th century team games and sports did not feature greatly in the school curriculum. Perhaps this was because society in general did not have much free time to participate in team sports due to long hours of work and Sundays being set aside for church going. Football was still largely a spectator sport in the late 19th century.

School reflected life and so sport was not considered important enough in the limited time available as pupils only had a few years of schooling. It seemed to be more necessary to pack in the three "rs". Pupils often walked five miles to school and some would have heavy work to do after their school day so sport for fitness was not so essential as it is today.

What was important was drill. This was like army training and was not just taught to build up body strength, but mentally to train young boys for a future army and later for girls to be fit mothers. There is plenty of evidence from studies done of recruits for the Boer War (1899-1901) being sent home because they were unfit and undernourished and too short. Something had to be done to improve the health of the nation.

As well as drill, strength and fitness were built up by using wooden "Indian" clubs and leapfrogging over "horses". School gyms were fitted with wall bars for climbing and "forms" for balancing. Games like "pirates" used all the new equipment - rubber mats , bean bags and plastic hoops. The hall was later marked out for netball and badminton.

In the 1950s and 60s Scottish Country Dancing was part of the winter curriculum in preparation for the Christmas parties.

Boys would line up on one side and girls on the other until forced to choose reluctant partners by the PE staff. Eightsome Reels, Dashing White Sergeants and Gay Gordons were all demonstrated and taught to many unwilling boys and girls. Some pupils, however, did enjoy this and dancing teams were organised to compete locally.

Football for boys and hockey for girls were the first regular sports. In 1929 there were five hockey teams and Hartfell,

Hockey 1967/68
Back Row L-R: Rosemary Sloan, Eileen Mackie, Carole Nutt, Heather Cameron, Karen Currie, Lynne Johnstone
Front Row L-R: Maureen Callendar, Mary Gass, Elizabeth Mitchell, Rosemary Carruthers, Julia Carruthers.

Lockerbie Academy Dance Team 1950
Back Row L-R: Hazel Oliver, James Wyllie, George Graham, Brian Nicol, Ian Dyer, Sergeant Kirkwood
Front Row L-R: Sheena Maltman, Moira Tracey, Ruby Byers and Sylvia Wylie.

captained by Jessie Burns, was the first winner on the shield.

Soon the school developed a house system and competitive team sports were encouraged. The school has several cabinets full of cups and shields which have been awarded through the decades for these sports.

The original names of the girls' houses were named after the hills in Annandale - Hartfell, Criffel, Queensberry, Skiddaw and Quhytewoollen. The boys' houses were named after the rivers- Tweed, Esk and the existing Annan (blue); Dryfe (green); Milk (yellow) and Kirtle (red). (They are now mixed sex houses).

3rd year Hockey team 1967
Back Row L-R: Allyson Reid, Mary Thompson, Vera Armstrong, Anne Wells, Lynna Baxter, Mrs Jan Geekie
Front Row L-R: Jill Jackson, Irene Wilson, Liz Richardson, Anne Morton, Margaret Thomson

1946 Football
Back Row L-R: Johnstone Hetherington (HT), Rae Graham, Bert Coppola, Stewart Nicholson, Dave Morran, Ronnie Callander, John Mitchell, Alex Gordon (English teacher)
Front Row L-R: Willie Elliot, Billy Mundle, George Hunter, Ronnie Dow, John Davison, Dave McLeod.

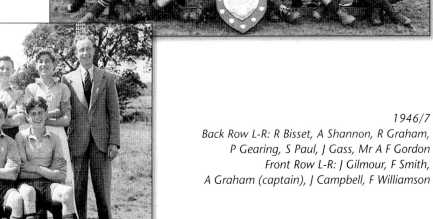

1946/7
Back Row L-R: R Bisset, A Shannon, R Graham, P Gearing, S Paul, J Gass, Mr A F Gordon
Front Row L-R: J Gilmour, F Smith, A Graham (captain), J Campbell, F Williamson

1949 Football team
Back Row L-R: Mr Gordon, John Clark, Bobbie Armstrong, Willie Edwards, Alec Hunter, John-, Bert Paterson, Douglas Armstrong.
Front Row L-R: Roy Thorbourn, Douglas Roxburgh, George Hume, Glen Graham, Murray Forbes.

Under 13 1965-66
Back Row: Ian Steele, P Murray, Andrew Hillier,
Gordon Greig, Keith Hunter, Brian Holt, Maitland Pollock
Front Row: Chris Headford, John Rogerson, A McKay,
R Earl, Tommy Devlin.

Under 13 football 1966-67
Back Row L-R: Andrew Hillier, William Gibson,
S Moffat, Robert Dodds, K Smith
Front Row: R Johnstone, Graham Till, R Little, Brian
Holt, J McDowall, J McCubbin, Roman Soltys.
Teacher: Arthur Johnstone.

Football Team 1969-70
Back Row L-R: J Bell, James Johnstone, R Stodart,
R Mason, D Thomson, R Watson, I little
Front Row: J Rae, G Dinwoodie,
Eddie Sharkey, S Ash, D Manson
Teacher: Arthur Johnstone

1971
Back Row L-R: 1, - Brany, 3, 4, 5, Scott Mason,
7, Finlay Geekie, Allan Burgess
Front Row: 1, Neil Jardine, Ian Gibson,
Robin Thomson, Norman McKay, 6, Tom Dow
Teachers: Bob McEwan, Chemistry
and Iain Robson, French.

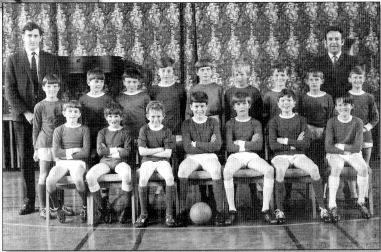

Under 13 football 1971-72
Back Row L-R: Robin Thompson, Norman McKay,
S Prisic, S Grieve, David Irving, Allan Burgess
Front Row: Irving McKay, MalcolmThorburn,
Kenny Robson, I Campbell, Ian Gibson.
Teacher: Arthur Johnstone

Lockerbie Academy Football Team 1972-3
Back Row L-R: Bill Reid,
Craig Davidson, 3, 4, 5, Derek Holt
Front Row: Willie Porteous, Ian Duddie,
Mike Riding, Jackie Bell, George -, Ian Cameron, 7, 8

A cricket team led by Alan Welsh (a teacher) was being coached for the first time in 1929 as well as Golf for both boys and girls. The teachers awarded the winners with golf balls.

Netball was seen as a girls' team sport and this was introduced in 1929 , but nowadays basketball has taken over in popularity for both sexes.

Note that the girls wore gym slips for their sports. In the early 20th century girls used to wear dark blue knickers often with their skirts tucked in to do Physical Education. Gym kits and shorts for girls became the norm by the 1960s.

Girls' Netball Team early 50s with PE teacher Margaret Condie

Kirtle House Netball Team 1969
Back Row L-R: Catherine -, Rosemary Carruthers,
Liz Farish, Anne Wells, Mrs Welsh
FrontRow: Anne Morton, Margot Miller, Anne Johnstone

It was then that badminton became a favourite for both boys and girls. George Hood and Matt Green did much to encourage the youngsters to enter county tournaments.

Badminton 1968
Back Row L-R: Fergus Donaldson, Kenny Anderson, David Bryson, Matt Green, Maitland Pollock, John Leopold, Gordon McNeil
Front Row L-R: Mary Spence, Anne Wells, Helen Common, Hazel Ritchie, Irene Wilson, Jill Jackson

Badminton 1969
Back Row L-R: Mr Hill, David Creelman, John Leopold, Kenny Anderson, John Rogerson, Mr Hood
Front Row L-R: Helen Common, Anne Wells, Mary Spence, Jill Jackson

In the 70s tennis was much encouraged by the PE teachers and pupil Andrew Moffat was in the team which won the South West Schools championships and went on to represent Lockerbie in Edinburgh at the Scottish Schools Championships.

The school is situated opposite the ice rink and pupils have taken advantage of this to develop curling as a relatively new school sport. Lockerbie became Scottish Schools Curling champions in 2006.

Athletics has been a strong feature in school sports' days and the school entered teams for the county sports.

Sports' Winners c1949
Front Row L-R: Alex Hunter, Doreen Walker, William Edwards
Back Row L-R: Vera Bell, Glen Graham and Betty Adamson

A sport or a field visit it depends on your point of view, but these youngsters and their teacher clearly enjoyed walking at Wamphray in the 1980s (page 72).

An archery club was set up largely by a third year pupil, Alan Sloan and by 1974 Golf was reintroduced by Mr Halliday.

Sailing in a school boat made from a kit by pupils was started in 1975 when Alistair Foggo finished first in the South West Schools Regatta. The school held the Penman Shield.

Many former pupils have said that they really appreciated the time and effort given by staff in extracurricular activities and today a huge variety of clubs are offered by staff: Hockey, Rugby, Football, Girls' Football. Badminton, Basketball, Curling, Gymnastics as well as the more sedentary Chess.

Lockerbie Curling Team 2006
Hannah Fleming, Claire Hamilton,
Anna Sloan, Megan Priestly.

County Sports Team with Shield for Relay June 1967
Back Row L-R: Roman Soltys, Maitland Pollock, Graham Till, Archie Jenkins,
Douglas Cameron, Denny Reid, Kenny Anderson, John Peart
Front Row L-R: Rosemary Sloan, Margaret Thomson, Audrey White, Lynna Baxter, David Nairn,
Anne Wells, Mr Harry Reid, Mary Caldow, Liz Richardson, Maureen Callander

Hill Walking Wamphray Glen March 1984
Included in photo are a number of teachers'
children, L-R: Fraser Sutcliffe, Alisdair
McEwan, Douglas Fountain,
Robin McTaggart, Neil Robson,
Fraser Hunter, David Russell,
Kenneth McKie crouching.
The Geography head of department
David Hughes led the group.

Lockerbie Academy
Rugby Team 1972-73
Back Row L-R: Gary Scott, 2, 3, 4,
Alan Rogerson, 5, 7, 8, Tom Russell
Front Row L-R: Jackie Bell, Bill Reid,
Aitken Smith, Mike Riding,
Craig Davidson,
Ian Cameron, George -, 8

Gaun up tae the big schule

Although it was not a particularly difficult transition for pupils from Lockerbie Primary "gaun up tae the Big Schule", it was and still is for pupils from the associated primaries.

In June 2007 I interviewed five pupils who had just completed their first year at Lockerbie Academy. I asked them about their feelings about the school before starting and whether these had changed a year later.

All five came from different primary schools. Lisa Irving came from the tiny Hottsbridge Primary so going to the big school was a bit worrying for her because of the sheer size and Karen Pollard from Lochmaben worried about getting lost .

Lauren Duffin from Brydekirk should have gone to nearby Annan Academy, but chose Lockerbie. She was the only pupil from her primary and so she was a bit lonely at first.

Saira Saleem started at Lockerbie with her big sister. They had come all the way from Pakistan and her main concern was the English language which she had learned, along with Urdu, at her large primary school. She need not have worried as her English is excellent.

The fifth pupil I interviewed was male and wanted to be anonymous. He came from Eaglesfield Primary and had heard stories of "heads being put down toilets". Thank fully these rumours were unfounded.

Another concern was forgetting the teachers' names. Having been used to their sole primary teacher, they were now to meet up to twelve different teachers a week. (I did not tell them that the teachers often have similar problems remembering names).

Coming from a small primary school is a big change for pupils - travelling to the school, the unfamiliar timetables, the size of the school in area and population and not knowing many people is daunting and also a wee bit frightening. Even though these first years knew some older pupils they were largely ignored by them and condemned as "freshers".

Now after a full year, they are all confident individuals and comfortable in their surroundings. They all said that now the school seemed smaller and that they enjoyed moving classes for the "better" range of subjects. The chance to build robots and learn Spanish were particularly appealing.

They preferred the black and white uniform to their brightly coloured Primary School sweatshirts and they thought the food was better.

One thing they didn't enjoy was homework!

They also said that whereas at primary they would play games at break times, there was little of that at Lockerbie other than the occasional impromptu football game (although there are plenty of after school clubs). Most pupils go to the assembly hall and sit and chat to friends whilst listening to the Music channels which are pre set on the widescreen plasma TV

Some go down the street, but the first years are denied this privilege

Lockerbie Academy has welcomed them and they have responded well to the "Big Schule" which has given them so many more opportunities.

Cartoon from The Pupils' Eye- a magazine which ran from 1991-1992
"1st day at new school"

Memories

Some pupils travel quite a distance to school. This has always been the case and this little poem written in 1929 by Jessie Andrews when she was in class 2A describes the journey taken to school by Lochmaben pupils- some of whom are named.

The Lochmaben Scholars

"1. By Caly 'bus each morning
  We travel to the school;
Our poor heads ache with learning,
  They are so very full.

2. There's Margaret with her laughter,
  And Muriel with her frown,
And Isa, who, alas, I think,
  Has started growing down.

3. There's Isobel McArthur,
  Who is rather thin and tall,
And Agnes Brown from Roselea-
  The Tom-boy of us all.

4. Next Sammy, ever smiling,
  Whether sun or rain,
And David, who, when we are sad,
  Will cheer us up again.

5. And then comes Barbara Grierson,
  She has a weary wait;
We stop for her at Halleath's Bridge,
  And she is seldom late.

6. But happy are our school days,
  And youth will always out;
We know the poor conductor
  Will forgive without a doubt."

John Nicholson has written a lengthy piece of prose about his first day at Lockerbie Academy in 1951. (See below). John went on to study Chemistry and became a science teacher and writer of text books. His younger sister, Elizabeth, has also written about her first days at Lockerbie when she went up to the big school in 1954.

"The Headmaster at the time was Mr Hetherington . His wife taught maths". Elizabeth was in the school hockey and netball teams, but her favourite subject was Music taught by Mr Blacklaw and the show that year was the Mikado in which her brother sang solo.

She particularly appreciated her English teacher, Mr Gordon: "Who let me recite Portia's The Quality of Mercy speech from the Merchant of Venice rather than Burns' To a Mouse like the other pupils - so sensitive of him because I had an English accent". Her most memorable teacher was Miss Tocher with whom she kept in touch until that lady died. Elizabeth's brother has also written about Tugela Tocher. (see appendix).

Lena Miller was a pupil in the early 1960s. She wrote that she enjoyed her school days, despite being rapped over the knuckles by the typing teacher for looking down at the keys;

being belted by "sweet" Mrs Hetherington for not listening and being scared stiff of her English teacher, Jenny Maxwell.

She recalled: " Matt Green - the heart throb, that is until replaced by his younger brother, Maurice." Lena began school in the old building and over the four years moved into the new one next to the gym which had showers! Her music teacher was George Tait who wrote a school musical in which she

George Reid Music teacher late 1950s

appeared singing "Old Joe Clark". Mr Tait also composed a song, "Hail to the Queen", for the Lockerbie Gala.

I remember my first day at the Academy in 1965. I was scared - scared most of my first year. We were divided up into streamed ability classes and the only pupils I knew in my new class were Ian Beck, Ian McDonald and a relatively new girl, Jean Moffat. It was a far cry from Lochmaben Primary where all of the year group had sat in the same classes for years. I thought I would never see my old friends again and in fact, some of them, I didn't. There was not much mingling between classes in those days.

The unfamiliar school, subjects and classmates was bad enough, but it seemed that I had got myself into a class which had the scariest teachers too. I quaked and quivered for a year!

After that initial start,however, I thoroughly enjoyed the next five years.

Calum Cameron, whose father and grandfather had both attended the school, wrote about school in the 1970s :

"On my first school day in my new uniform, I walked back to my house in Sydney Place via the market and fell in the midden. My mum made me undress on the back door step due to the smell - it was pretty bad as I remember and I had ruined my new uniform."

Pearl Gaitskill (nee Lindsay) remembered her first day at Lockerbie.

" It was bigger than even I could have imagined, and on the first Monday, first lesson after lunch was maths. Somehow I got separated from everyone else and was trying to find Room 35, Mrs Gordon's class. Well, I just couldn't find it, and, in the corridor was a rather stern teacher giving two boys a real telling-off. So being a rather non-confrontational kind of person, I decided to find someone else to ask. I think I toured the whole block and eventually, after about ten minutes, the route brought me back down to this very stern teacher. I summoned up every ounce of courage to ask this teacher where Room 35 was - and she just swung her arm up, not missing a beat in the telling off - and pointed straight at the door at which she was standing! I behaved like a little angel in her class after that, I can tell you!!"

Another pupil from the 1980s Jason Smith, now an army sergeant, thought the school had great teachers and characters: Ma Miller- honest and straight to the point; Mrs Strawthorn - a rock; Dr Oswald; Mr Miller; Mr Buckle (not too bad at football); Joe Boardman and the inspirational Mrs Lewis.

A new school

"For nearly six years I had been a pupil at Ardeer Primary School in Ayrshire, not far from a slag heap, an unprotected mine shaft, and the ICI factory where my dad had spent happy years as an explosives expert. Then he was moved to Dumfries, and we moved to Broadholm, a lovely house way out in the country. To get to school we walked across fields for half a mile to Applegarth Town, and from there we went to Lockerbie Academy in style, in a taxi no less.

The only thing that the Academy had in common with Ardeer Primary was red sandstone. Everything else was different. It was large and energetic, full of Big Boys and Girls. I felt very small.

Elisabeth and I were taken past the sandstone building, down a short steep slope, and into a concrete classroom on the right. Primary Six for her, Primary Seven for me and a young teacher with dark hair, a bright dress, and authority. Miss Oliver. She sat me at the front, next to Billy Airlie who welcomed me with an open grin.

Sitting near the front took some getting used to. I was bottom of the class. I had always sat in the back row with a group of clever girls and Jimmy. Like me, Jimmy was a voracious reader from a home full of books, music, the wireless and conversation, and like me never felt the need to make any effort. Lockerbie was different. Behind me was a confident group of children who knew each other and what they had to do. They belted out unheard of hymns first thing in the morning. 'We are trampling out the vineyards where the grapes of wrath are stored!' In clear voices, without the heavy tones of North Ayrshire, they recited chunks of Bible I did not know. Some of it was so beautiful, about charity, about seeing through a glass darkly, about putting away childish things.

I was weak at mental arithmetic, shot at us like a cold shower straight after God, doing us good, keeping us on our toes. '20 pounds of sugar at seven pence halfpenny a pound, hands-up don't shout out.' I would love to have shouted out, to hear in my head the clear voice from behind which said 'twelve and six' and only God knew how. Miss Oliver fired more numerical volleys before settling us down to serious work, like Areas, Bills and Compositions. Behind me heads were down, although there were always secret diversions from characters like James Rae and Billy Irving.

My first fight was with James Rae. I knew that a fight would happen eventually. It always did when I changed school. Not only was I new, I was half English, and despite my best efforts I probably sounded posh. Why we came to blows I cannot remember. I lost but only just. It started in the Boys Toilets. Perhaps I had mocked his capacity to pee high up the wall. We were firm friends after that.

Within weeks I felt at home, still at the front, but secure in Billy's immediate friendship. His twin, Greta, sat nearby. Greta was pretty, had long fair curling hair, full of fun and showing early signs of womanhood. She was the first girl at Lockerbie I took a fancy to.

She and her girl friends must have noticed. There was a teasing, a gentle mocking, a collective come-on, a seduction. One sunny dinnertime we gathered on the far side of the football pitch, out of sight of school in the long grass. 'She wants to kiss you, come on, kiss her!' So we wriggled on our tummies through warm meadow-grass until our faces were inches apart and kiss we did. Just once, swift and sweet. Then we retreated into childhood and the safety of our friends. I never kissed another girl in all my time at Lockerbie."

by John Nicholson

Appendix 1
A
Miss Tocher

Tugela Tocher was named after the Battle of the Tugela River in the Boer War. Tugela, Thukela in Zulu, means 'the frightening or startling one'. She lived up to her name.

We knew nothing of this when we were eleven, just that she had a strange name, which from a safe distance we shortened to Tougie. Known and feared the length of Lockerbie, the name 'Tougie' was essentially Lowland Scots. It embodied that sharp tug of hair that pulled lads into order and her toughness, her capacity to cow the largest of louts in a nanosecond.

This took some doing. Tougie was tiny, less than 5 foot tall. What she lacked in height she made up for in gristle and aggression. Had she been male she would have made a great marauding hooker or scrum-half, knocking over opponents twice her size. Being female gave her an even greater edge. If she ever hit you, you could never hit her back.

Armoured in her tweed suit or ancient lab-coat, she ruled her class and all around her with a box-wood metre stick. She would slap it on her demonstration bench and sometimes on our heads, moving round the semicircle of children ranged on stools in front of her. "Define density!" she would order, and if we could not remember 'mass per unit volume' the box-wood would descend. 'You must know your definitions, learn your definitions!' Once, having shattered a stick beyond use, she sent me to her store cupboard to find a replacement. There was one, immaculate inside a box of shattered splintered remnants. How many definitions had been learned on the end of those? For me the answer was simple. None.

Her parade-ground methods did not work for me, but she had others that did. From the first day in her lab she let me do science, so that I saw science as an exploration, an activity, much more than definitions to be recalled. She stimulated and she fascinated, letting me do things that now would not be allowed – feeling the asbestos fire-blanket in ignorance of asbestosis, allowing ether to evaporate from our fingers to feel its chilling demand for latent heat, rolling a gleaming bead of mercury in our palms, a molten metal unable to burn. She boiled water in a large metal can, screwed the lid on, and let it cool. I watched entranced as it collapsed, crushed into twisted steel.

She explained and demonstrated how this happened, using a pump to suck air from between two close-fitting hemispheres of brass until they stuck fast. She told us of Magdeburg and his scaled-up version so that I could imagine his teams of horses competing with air pressure to pull the vacuum-filled, the nothing-filled shells apart.

She also challenged. 'Why doesn't air crush you?'

'We have air inside us Miss?'

'In your lungs yes Nicholson, but what about your legs?'

I imagined them shrinking and twisting until she explained the balancing effect of blood pressure. Not yet in my teens, I began to see connections, to glimpse cause and effect in the world around me, and to be excited by the capacity of science

to lift the lid on life. Not only that, my dad was a chemist. Maybe I could be one too.

I also thought I might become a professional actor, an international rugby player, a star of some kind. I wrote as much in Miss Downie's English class. "What I Will Be When I Grow Up." Being 'Something' would just happen one day, like shaving, without effort. Life was a playground, dreams would materialise.

Miss Tocher knew otherwise. She knew, before I did, that something would have to be done about me.

A Belting

At thirteen I had a serious problem. Disorder. Unlike John Hay, June and all the other girls I could not keep my science file neat and tidy. My pages constantly fell out, the twin holes in the paper torn by forces that did not seem to attack theirs. They had neatly ruled double-lines of ink under each heading. Somehow I never even had a ruler. They had pristine pages of neat hand-writing. I had blots and stains spreading across mine like a rash, pursuing the inky spider which had apparently stumbled its way along the lines. I had the 50s equivalent of a computer virus. I could not help it, blots and stains seemed just to happen, an effect beyond my control.

One day Miss Tocher lost patience. 'Get out of here Nicholson, stand outside the door and wait for me!' I was in for a roasting so bad, I told myself, that she did not want the rest of the class to share my embarrassment.

It was much worse than that. She came through the lab door, and closed it gently behind her in an atmosphere of total silence. Perhaps the class had seen what I now saw, the coiled leather of her strap, one she hardly ever used, perhaps had never used with our class. It uncoiled, curved in her right hand, split ends menacing, the tongue of a snake.

'I have had enough! Hold out your hand!'

Holding out my hand was not new to me - it happened every week with Miss Waller - and might be better than a verbal attack. I extended my right hand.

'Out a bit, to the right!'

Then she hit me. It really hurt. As my palm swelled and reddened so did my resentment grow. I had not been disobedient or insolent, I had merely blotted my file. That's all. This was unfair, unjust.

'Now the left!' This time it hurt more.

'And again!'

I was shocked and hurt as hard leather smacked into me a third time. I expect my face was a red as either hand. Tears of rage smarted behind my eyes. I tried to keep control. I could not lose face on my return.

For the rest of the period I kept my head down, wondering how on earth I was supposed to write cleanly and correctly with swollen hands. Mouth and mind set in a straight line, I did not look to my classmates for attention or sympathy. In icy silence I kept my counsel.

The pain and swelling diminished, but not the anger, not the resentment. They grew like mushrooms in my mind, made all the worse because Miss Tocher was a teacher I respected, almost liked. For the first time ever I complained of my belting to my mother.

The Word

I never complained as a rule of course, because I had always asked for it until now. I would have been ashamed to admit to my parents what a toe-rag I could be. 'Just for blotting your file?' asked my Mum, and when I nodded said 'I think your Dad should know about this.' Normally I would want to have kept the old man out of this sort of thing, but on this occasion was all for it. When he came home I told him the story, and he responded with sympathy, concern and (oh help) with action. "I think I need to talk with that woman – what did you say her name was? Right.' Things were serious, but looking up. He was going to take the redoubtable Tougie to task, sort her out as only my Dad could, and vindicate my sense of injustice. Tongue protruding from the side of his mouth – always a sign of focussed concentration – he picked up the 'phone. I listened in anticipation as he spoke to the operator.

'Yes, the name is Tocher, Miss Tocher, she lives in Lockerbie.' There was a pause.

'Ex-directory you say? Mmm. Then to me.

'What's the name of the Head at the Academy?' He tried again

'I want to speak to Mr. Johnston Hetherington.'

Things were heading out of control. I heard him in conversation, saw his grin. 'Got it!' He phoned again.

'Miss Tocher? ... Good ... Doctor Nicholson here. I want a Word.'

'Having a Word' was a euphemism. I had experienced it many times. Would The Word sort out Miss Tocher as it could me? As I eavesdropped it became clear that the person having the Word was Miss Tocher, not my Dad. 'Really!' he said, 'I see… .Mmm….. Oh, he did not tell me that!' The tone became conciliatory, there was even a chuckle. Adults were consorting, conspiring and I was doomed. After an age, the phone clicked back into its cradle and my Dad came through. 'John. A word. I doubt she hit you hard enough. It wasn't just the ink blots, it's everything else. She wants to see you tomorrow.'

I cannot now remember how or when I saw her, just that I did. The ink blots, she told me, were the final straw, the last of a long list of things done and undone. I did not pay enough attention, listen, or concentrate, and certainly did not apply myself. I had ability and I was wasting it. She wanted me to succeed but I could only do this if I helped myself, starting by keeping my notes neat and in good order. She left me with the feeling that despite everything she almost liked me and wanted me to do well.

Two years later I came across that science file. The first part was a disgraceful inky mess: the final part written, apparently, by someone else. The transformation was miraculous, as if a deity had said 'take up thy pen and write, take up thy ruler and rule.' The pages were splash-free, the writing legible and on the lines. The dots on each i and on the stroke of each t were level, smack on the imaginary lines I had first met in Primary 3. Dates and headings were neatly and doubly underlined. The drawings, in pencil, were immaculate. At university, seven years after the Tougie treatment, my wife to be saw my chemistry notes, not the ones I scribbled in lectures, but the researched and developed versions I wrote up afterwards. She was astonished. Apparently in other respects I was as scruffy and disorganised as I had been at Lockerbie - but not in my work, and not in the lab. This was territory I had learned to feel at home in, was compelled to manage and to make my own. Who says corporal punishment does not work?

Well I do for one. It was not the hard flexing leather that had turned me round. It was the softer strength of someone who cared despite appearances, who saw potential, but who used the harsher methods of her time. Her approach was reinforced by her response to my Insect Collection – but that is another story.

by John Nicholson

Appendix 1
B

The Insect Collection

In 1ABC we had to do a science project. We could make a collection of pressed plants or insects or keep a nature diary. There was a prize in each category. We knew this early in Autumn, and had to hand it in after the Easter holidays. All the time in the world, so I forgot about it.

In Spring I saw what I should have been doing. Girls brought specimens into school to show each other, neatly pressed snowdrops, violets, and primroses, mounted, labelled and dated on sheets of pristine paper. We boys were unmoved, although one or two admitted that they had started. So one weekend I picked what flowers I could find from the wintry ground, shoved them between layers of Bronco under some heavy books, and left them to get on with it.

Come Easter there was little to show, just floppy dehyrating plants, staining the lavatory paper with smudges of green and yellow. I was running out of time.

A Nature Diary? For a moment or two I thought about making one up. However I lacked the little blue jotter all Diarists had been issued with, and anyway cheating was not done. Not with Miss Tocher anyway. There was only one thing to do. I had to make an Insect Collection. I lived in the country, insects would be everywhere wouldn't they?

They were thin on the window sills. Dozy blue-bottles which had survived the winter did not survive the cruel stab of a pin from my Mum's sewing basket, right through the thorax. I collected at least four kinds of fly.

When do four flies become a collection? The Children's Encyclopaedia showed row after row of butterflies and I had not found one. I could not even find a chrysalis to warm up in hope. I was in trouble.

Then a brainwave – spiders! The disused stables of Broadholm were full of them, stretching their webs to catch dust, insects, and the occasional sunbeam through dilapidated roofs. I climbed into places un-trod and forbidden to find them.

I made a fine haul of moths, long expired in a frantic tangle, desiccated, sucked dry. I brushed and blew them into some respectability, like very old ladies rescued from a morgue to be dressed in fading gowns for a final tableau. I needed at least another 12 pins.

I also needed a display box. The encyclopaedia showed me a wooden box, mahogany with brass hinges and black velvet interior. I used a small cardboard box instead.

I took my collection to school with some relief. The labels were un-researched, written in blotchy ink, the lines of corpses still with traces of old web, but it was an insect collection, and as it happened, the only one. 'You'll get a prize!' said David Latto, my pall from Halleaths across the Annan. The possibility excited me. I had never won a prize at Lockerbie.

The collection looked out of place among the neat pile of blue nature diaries and impressive folders of flowers, but all I had to do was wait. The prize would be mine.

'There will be no prize for an insect collection this year,' Miss Tocher told me, in private, two days later. There was no anger in her voice, only resignation and a sigh. 'I am disappointed in you. You can do so much better than this. Off you go.'

This was worse than the belt, worse than not having a prize. This was a moment of truth. As I write this, more than fifty tears later, I feel what I felt then, the sadness, the tightness in the chest that signals tears. She knew I could do better. She wanted me to do better. I had to do better. I could not let her down again. Or me.

Somewhere in a cardboard box I have a small worn note book. It has hard blue covers. It is full of neat notes in ink and sketches in pencil, detailed observations I made day-after-day the following year. And on the desk in front of me is my Observer's Book of British Birds. Inside is a certificate, signed in the immaculate hand of Johnstone Hetherington, Principal Teacher, Lockerbie Academy July 1954. It was presented by Science Department Staff, the prize for my Nature Diary.

by John Nicholson

Appendix 2
Odds and ends

In Dumfriesshire the name for a Headteacher is Rector. There have been no female headteachers at Lockerbie.

Lockerbie Academy has its own Student radio station run by the S3 and S4.

The intercom system for school notices still exists, but now there is in addition a digital display board in the cafeteria which shows the news of the day.

The school crest - the flying spur encircling an open book is adapted from the Johnstone Family Crest. (Lord of Annandale) and the motto is Numquam non Paratus - never unprepared. (see back page)

School uniform included a red and yellow striped tie for juniors and black with school crest for seniors.

5th and 6th year pupils finish school now with a Prom. They dress up, long dresses, and kilts and arrive in limo's. Very Hollywood!

The 13 associated primary schools are:-

Applegarth, Eaglesfield, Hightae, Hoddam, Hottsbridge, Hutton, Johnstonebridge, Kirkpatrick Fleming, Lochmaben, Lockerbie, Nethermill, St Mungo and Tundergarth.

The dialect of the pupils was very "pure" in the 1880s - the old Border vernacular, but teachers insisted that the children would have to go out into the world after they left school and would have to speak like the rest of the country. A teacher of English, however, reported that: "The vowel sounds which are so beautiful in a Border ballad did not suit the lines of Gray's Elegy so we substituted The Cottar's Saturday Night for repetition."

Up until fairly recently Scots' children had two languages - that of the school and that of the playground.

The Syracuse Scholarship students are:-

1990/91	Kathryn Grant & Fiona Griffin
1991/92	Colin Combe & John Wallace
1992/93	Kirsteen Scott & Moira Weatherup
1993/94	Jennifer Coates & Richard Irving
1994/95	Gareth McIntyre & Louise Wilson
1995/96	Katrina Bogie & Lucy Gibson
1996/97	Kerry Currie & David Thomson
1997/98	Gavin Fleming & Helen Greig
1998/99	Fiona Drysdale & Alison Younger
1999/00	Deborah Allbrooke & Fiona Sewell
2000/01	Gemma Ritchie & Stephen Armstrong
2001/02	Claire Speedie & Fiona Stevenson
2002/03	Ruth McNay & Andrew McClune
2003/04	Erin McLaughlin & Jamie Graham
2004/05	Beth Marchant & Laura Smith
2005/06	Allan Berry & Angus Moodie
2006/07	Joanna Graham & Adam Brooks

Kirsten & Moira, 1992

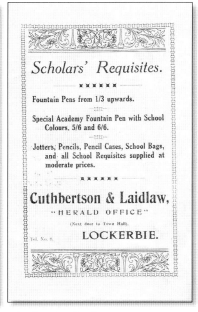

Adverts from 1929 from the "Lockardian"

The prefect badge has changed only slightly over the years and the prefect system has been around for most of the 20th century. Duties included patrolling toilets and corridors in breaks and keeping order at the doors when the bell rang at lunchtime.

Prefects 1965/66
Back Row L-R: A Henderson, R Shannon, D Hall, M Thom, N Cameron, R Riding, W Frame, C McKay, P Saville
Middle Row: E Ritchie, A Gibson, J Horsburgh, M Mollins, A McLean, J Ritchie, E Halliday, M Bell
Front Row: M Anderson, G Traill (Head Girl) Mr Miller, Mr Anderson, Mrs Fraser, W Jackson (Head Boy), L Nicol

Assistant Prefects 1965/66
Back Row L-R: I McQueen, D Nairn, R Macfarlane, R Davidson, J Rogerson, F Donaldson, K Lockhart
Middle Row: A Logan, A McNeish, H Common, S Bryden, E A Rodger, C Munro, M Roberts, S Jardine
Front Row: T Woods, J McIntosh, Mr Miller, Mr Anderson, Mrs Fraser, M Wright, J Peart

Prefects 1967/68
Back Row L-R: Kenneth Anderson, Niall Weatherstone, Douglas Cameron, Scott Wylie,
Wm Greenshields, Brian McNaught, Robert Spence, Keith Laurie, David Bryson
Middle Row: Janet Miller, Catherine Young, Kathleen Reid, Mary Cameron, Elizabeth-Ann Rodger,
Christine Munro, Elizabeth Rogerson, Margot Miller, Julia Kulik.
Front Row: John Stewart, Jean Richardson, Mr Gronbach, Mr Anderson, Mrs Fraser, John Glover, Joan Wightman

Assistant Prefects 1967/68
Back Row L-R: Ian Beck, Alan Copeland, Keith Hunter, Morris McSkimming, William Wightman, Gordon Greig, William Chambers.
Middle Row: Margaret Crossan, Agnes Little, Karen Currie, Aileen Laurie, Valerie Martin, Margaret Smith, Sandra Little.
Front Row: John Rogerson, Laura De Luca, Mr Gronbach, Mr Anderson, Mrs Fraser, Maitland Pollock, Maureen Callander.

Prefects 1968/69
Back Row L-R: Roger Chard, David Macdonald, Robert Spence, John Leopold, Andrew Rogerson, Tom Roehricht, Graham Weatherstone
Middle Row: Carol Bell, Elizabeth Richardson, Lynna Baxter, Catherine Young,
Catherine Forrester, Elizabeth Johnstone, Margot Miller, Kathleen Reid, Allyson Reid
Front Row: Irene Hendrie, Elizabeth-Ann Rodger, Mr Gronbach, Mr Anderson, Mrs Fraser, Niall Weatherstone, Kenneth Anderson

Assistant Prefects 1968/69
Back Row L-R: Michael Malone, David Wells, Andrew Mackie, Stewart Moffat, Graham Till, Robert McNay, Kevin Smith, John Milligan
Middle Row: Janice Ferguson, Pamela Dempster, Elma Davidson, Margaret Kean, Sandra Rowe, June Smith
Front Row: Donna Thompson, Dorothy Galloway, Mr Gronbach, Mr Anderson, Mrs Fraser, Margaret Gray, Jean Gray

Assistant Prefects 1966/67
Back Row L-R: Alistair McKay, Thomas Devlin, Maitland Pollock, John Peart, Douglas Robson, Michael Jamieson
Middle Row: Barbara Maxwell, Elizabeth Richardson, Nancy Johnstone, Richenda Brown, Anne Wells, Mary Spence, Frances Ross
Front Row: David Nairn, 2, M Gronbach, Mr Anderson (Rector), Mrs Fraser, Archie Jenkins, 7.

The Author

The author is a former pupil of Lochmaben Primary ("A Guid Wee Schule" pub.2005) and Lockerbie Academy. She studied at Edinburgh University and later at Heriot-Watt.

She has taught History for many years alongside researching family histories and has now returned to her native Lochmaben where she hopes to continue teaching, researching and writing.

She is married with one grown-up daughter.

She would like to hear from readers who may be able to provide missing names and - perhaps - corrections for the photos. (She apologises in advance for any mistaken identities.) Further photos (which would be returned) may also be sent as these would all prove useful in the event of a second editon.

Contact Isabelle directly at:
gow.isabelle@yahoo.com
or via the school.

Isabelle Gow,
Author

Graham Herbert,
Present Rector of Lockerbie Academy